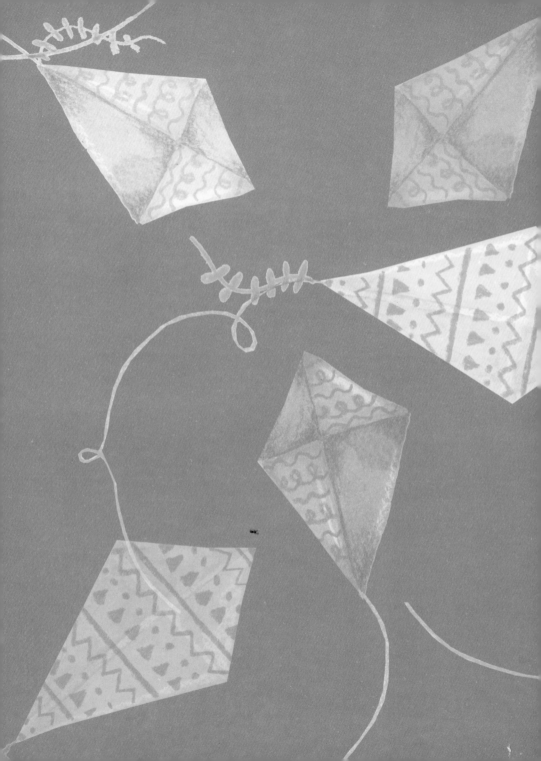

To:

_____

From:

_____

Date:

_____

Devotions for Beginning Readers

Crystal Bowman and Christy Lee Taylor

A Division of Thomas Nelson Publishers

NASHVILLE   MEXICO CITY   RIO DE JANEIRO

Published in Nashville, Tennessee, by Tommy Nelson. Tommy Nelson is an imprint of Thomas Nelson. Thomas Nelson is a registered trademark of HarperCollins Christian Publishing, Inc.

Published in association with the literary agency of Ann Spangler and Company, 1420 Pontiac Road, S.E., Grand Rapids, Michigan, 49506.

Tommy Nelson titles may be purchased in bulk for educational, business, fund-raising, or sales promotional use. For information, please e-mail SpecialMarkets@ThomasNelson.com

Unless otherwise noted, Scripture quotations are taken from INTERNATIONAL CHILDREN'S BIBLE®. © 1986, 1988, 1999 by Thomas Nelson. All rights reserved.

Scripture quotations marked NIrV are taken from Scripture taken from the Holy Bible, NEW INTERNATIONAL READER'S VERSION®.Copyright © 1996, 1998 Biblica. All rights reserved throughout the world. Used by permission of Biblica. Scripture quotations marked NLT are taken from *Holy Bible*, New Living Translation. © 1996. Used by permission of Tyndale House Publishers, Inc., Wheaton, Illinois 60189. All rights reserved. Scripture quotations marked NIV are taken from Holy Bible, New International Version®, NIV®. Copyright © 1973, 1978, 1984, 2011 by Biblica, Inc.™ Used by permission of Zondervan. All rights reserved worldwide. *www.zondervan.com*. Scripture quotations marked ESV are taken from the ENGLISH STANDARD VERSION. © 2001 by Crossway Bibles, a division of Good News Publishers. Scripture quotations marked CEV are taken from THE CONTEMPORARY ENGLISH VERSION. © 1991 by the American Bible Society. Used by permission. Scripture quotations marked GNT are taken from THE GOOD NEWS TRANSLATION. © 1976, 1992 by The American Bible Society. Used by permission. All rights reserved. Scripture quotations marked ERV are taken from Easy-to-Read Version Copyright ©2006 World Bible Translation Center.

Library of Congress Cataloging-in-Publication Data

Bowman, Crystal, author.
  Devotions for beginning readers / Crystal Bowman and Christy Lee Taylor.
    pages cm
  Audience: Ages 4-8.
    ISBN 978-0-529-10401-4 (hardcover) 1. Devotional literature--Juvenile literature. 2. Children--Prayers and devotions. 3. Christian life--Juvenile literature. I. Taylor, Christy Lee, author. II. Bible. English. International Children's Bible. III. Title.
  BV4870.B636 2014
  242.62--dc23

2014018803

Printed in China
16 17 18 TIMS 6 5

Mfr: TIMS / Shenzhen, China / SEPTEMBER 2016 / PPO #9418425

Note to Parents

Dear Parents,

We are so happy you have chosen *Devotions for Beginning Readers* to share with a special child in your life! Learning to read is a milestone for every child and opens the door to unlimited knowledge. When children begin to read on their own, it is important for them to read books that are specifically designed for beginning readers. The words in this book have been carefully selected to adhere to the reading vocabulary of young readers. Nearly every word is geared to the reading level of pre-kindergarten through second grade. We have also included many words from the Dolch sight word list to enable young readers to master these standard vocabulary words.

The use of short, straightforward sentences allows for pleasurable reading and easier comprehension. In each devotion you will see "Today's Word," which will be used in the devotion to help children build their vocabulary. Our hope is that children will gain reading confidence as they turn the pages and enjoy the kid-friendly devotions and illustrations.

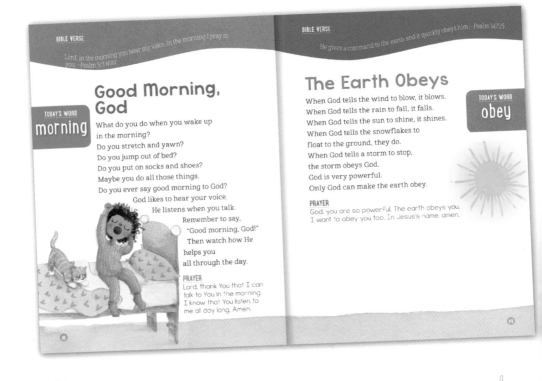

BIBLE VERSE

Lord, in the morning you hear my voice. In the morning I pray to you.—Psalm 5:3 NRSV

Good Morning, God

TODAY'S WORD
morning

What do you do when you wake up in the morning?
Do you stretch and yawn?
Do you jump out of bed?
Do you put on socks and shoes?
Maybe you do all those things.
Do you ever say good morning to God?
God likes to hear your voice.
He listens when you talk.
Remember to say,
"Good morning, God!"
Then watch how He helps you all through the day.

PRAYER
Lord, thank You that I can talk to You in the morning. I know that You listen to me all day long. Amen.

BIBLE VERSE

He gives a command to the earth and it quickly obeys him.—Psalm 147:15

The Earth Obeys

When God tells the wind to blow, it blows.
When God tells the rain to fall, it falls.
When God tells the sun to shine, it shines.
When God tells the snowflakes to float to the ground, they do.
When God tells a storm to stop, the storm obeys God.
God is very powerful.
Only God can make the earth obey.

TODAY'S WORD
obey

PRAYER
God, you are so powerful. The earth obeys you. I want to obey you too. In Jesus's name, amen.

The topics included in the devotions address issues from everyday life. The positive and encouraging messages will help children grow in their understanding of God and how much He loves them. *Devotions for Beginning Readers* can be used at mealtime, bedtime, or anytime you want to spend some quality time reading with your child. You can listen as your child reads the devotions word by word or take turns reading them to each other. As your child becomes familiar with the words, he or she will soon be able to read it with little or no help—a big accomplishment! No matter when or how you use this book, our prayer is that *Devotions for Beginning Readers* will be something your child will want to read over and over again!

Many blessings,
Crystal Bowman and Christy Lee Taylor

God's Big Love

TODAY'S WORD

big

Can you think of something that is big?

The sky is very big.

An ocean is very big.

A mountain is very big.

Did you know that God's love is big too?

It is bigger than the sky.

It is bigger than an ocean.

And it is bigger than a mountain.

God loves you all the time.

He will never stop loving you.

God's love is very big!

PRAYER

Dear God, thank You for Your big love. I know that You love me all the time. In Jesus' name, amen.

[Jesus] said, "I am the light of the world. The person who follows me will never live in darkness." —John 8:12

Follow the Light

Have you ever used a flashlight?
A flashlight helps you to see in the dark.
It shines a beam of light so you
can see where you are going.
A flashlight helps you to be safe.
Jesus is like a flashlight.
He shows us where to go.
He helps us to see what is
best for us.
Jesus shows us how to live
so we can be safe.

TODAY'S WORD

flashlight

PRAYER
Dear Jesus, thank You for being my light in this world. Please keep me safe. In Jesus' name, amen.

God created human beings in his own image. —Genesis 1:27 NLT

In God's Image

TODAY'S WORD

image

Everything God made is good.
But people are extra special.
God made people in His image.
That means we can think and talk.
We can laugh and sing.
We can read the Bible and
we can talk to God.
Animals can't do that, but people can.
You were made in God's image.
And that makes you extra special.

PRAYER

Dear God, thank You for making me
in Your image.
That makes me feel very special!
In Jesus' name, amen.

You saw my body as it was formed. —Psalm 139:16

Before You Were Born

Parents do not know what their baby
will look like until it is born.
Will it have curly hair?
Will it have brown eyes or blue eyes?
Only God knows what babies will look like.
He sees babies as they are being formed.
God saw you before you were born.
And He liked what He saw!

PRAYER

Dear God. You saw me before I was born. Thank
You for creating me. In Jesus' name. amen.

"God even knows how many hairs are on your head."—Matthew 10:30

Too Many to Count

count

What color is your hair?

Is it brown or black?

Is it red or yellow?

Is your hair long or short?

Can you count all the hairs on your head?

No way!

You have too many hairs to count.

But guess what?

God knows what color your hair is.

He knows how long it is.

And He knows how many hairs are on your head.

He has counted them all!

PRAYER

Dear God, I am happy that You know so much about me. Help me to know more about You. In Jesus' name, amen.

If any of you needs wisdom, you should ask God for it.—James 1:5

Ask for Wisdom

Do you want to be smart?

It is good to study so you can be smart.

But it is also good to be wise.

Being wise means you make good choices.

Being wise means you do the right
thing at the right time.

God can help you to be wise.

All you need to do is ask Him.

TODAY'S WORD

wise

PRAYER

Dear God, I want to be wise. Please give me lots
of wisdom today. In Jesus' name, amen.

I call to you, God, and you answer me. Listen to me now.
Hear what I say. —Psalm 17:6

Never Too Busy

TODAY'S WORD

listen

God makes the sun come up
in the morning.
He makes the clouds move
through the sky.
He watches over the birds
and the flowers.
He watches over His people.
But God is never too busy
to listen to you.
You can ask Him any question.
You can talk to Him anytime.
You can tell Him anything.
And He will always listen.

PRAYER

Dear God, thank You that You always listen to me
when I talk to You. In Jesus' name, amen.

He who guards you never sleeps. —Psalm 121:3

Up All Night

It's fun to play during the day.
But at night we need to sleep.
Babies need to sleep.
Kids need to sleep.
Grown-ups need to sleep too.
But God never sleeps.
The Bible says that God
watches over you all night.
You can sleep while God
stays awake.
Before you go to sleep,
say thank You to God for
watching over you.

TODAY'S WORD

sleep

PRAYER
Dear God, thank You
for watching over me
all night long. In Jesus'
name, amen.

BIBLE VERSE

LORD, in the morning you hear my voice. In the morning I pray to you. —Psalm 5:3 NIrV

Good Morning, God

What do you do when you wake up in the morning?
Do you stretch and yawn?
Do you jump out of bed?
Do you put on socks and shoes?
Maybe you do all those things.
Do you ever say good morning to God?
God likes to hear your voice.
He listens when you talk.
Remember to say,
"Good morning, God!"
Then watch how He helps you all through the day.

PRAYER

Lord, thank You that I can talk to You in the morning. I know that You listen to me all day long. In Jesus' name, amen.

He gives a command to the earth and it quickly obeys him.—Psalm 147:15

The Earth Obeys

When God tells the wind to blow, it blows.
When God tells the rain to fall, it falls.
When God tells the sun to shine, it shines.
When God tells the snowflakes to
float to the ground, they do.
When God tells a storm to stop,
the storm obeys God.
God is very powerful.
Only God can make the earth obey.

TODAY'S WORD

obey

PRAYER

God, You are so powerful. The earth obeys You.
I want to obey You too. In Jesus' name, amen.

I am sure that your goodness and love will follow me all the days of my life. —Psalm 23:6 NIrV

Goodness and Love

Do you have a brother or sister
who follows you around the house?
Do you have a pet that follows
you outside when you go for a walk?
The Bible tells us about something
that follows us.
It's called goodness and love.
God is good and God is love.
God's goodness and love follow you
everywhere you go.

PRAYER

Dear God, thank You
for Your goodness and
love. Thank You for Your
promise to follow me. In
Jesus' name, amen.

This is the day that the LORD has made. Let us rejoice and be glad today. —Psalm 118:24

Be Glad Today

You can be glad because God made today.

God made today for you to enjoy.

God makes every day for you to enjoy.

Every day is not your birthday.

Every day is not Christmas.

But you can be glad every day

because God made it for you.

Are you glad today?

Say thank You to God for making this day.

PRAYER

Dear God, thank You for today. I will be glad today because You made this day for me. In Jesus' name, amen.

God's Gifts

TODAY'S WORD

gifts

Birthday gifts are fun to open.

Did you know that God gives us gifts too?

His gifts do not come in boxes.

They are already open.

God gives us food and sunshine.

He gives us our family and friends.

Are you healthy and strong?

Those are gifts too.

God's gifts are called blessings.

He gives us blessings every day.

You don't have to wait until

your birthday!

PRAYER

Dear God, thank You for all the gifts and blessings You give me every day. In Jesus' name, amen.

Create in me a clean heart, O God. —Psalm 51:10 NLT

Clean on the Inside

TODAY'S WORD

clean

Mud pies are fun to make.
But they are messy and dirty.
When you are finished, you need to
wash your hands with soap and water.
Soap and water makes us clean
on the outside.
Did you know you can be clean on the
inside too?
You don't need soap and water.
You just need to ask Jesus to take
away your sins.
Then you can be clean inside and out.

PRAYER

Dear Jesus, thank You for taking away my sins
and making me clean on the inside. In Jesus'
name, amen.

Lily

BIBLE VERSE

I have given you all the trees whose fruits have seeds in them. They will be food for you. —Genesis 1:29

All Kinds of Trees

TODAY'S WORD

trees

God made all kinds of trees.
Some are tall and skinny.
Some are bushy with lots of leaves.
Trees start from a tiny seed.
They need water and food to grow
just like you do.
Some trees give us fresh fruit to eat.
Do you like apples and peaches?
The next time you bite into some
fruit, remember that God made the trees.

PRAYER

Dear God, thank You for all the trees You made and for fresh fruit to eat. In Jesus' name. amen.

22

The LORD's love never ends. His mercies never stop. —Lamentations 3:22

It Never Ends

When you read a book,
the story comes to an end.
When you go to a football game,
the game comes to an end.
When it is summer, the summer
will end, and then it will be fall.
Almost everything ends.
Do you want to know something that
never ends?
God's love.
His love for you will last forever.
Everything about God lasts forever.
It never ends.

TODAY'S WORD

end

PRAYER
Dear God, thank
You that Your love
for me never
ends. In Jesus'
name, amen.

God's Many Names

There are over one hundred names for God in the Bible!

He is called Shepherd because He cares for us.

He is called Rock because He protects us.

He is called Teacher because He teaches us.

He is called Comforter because He comforts us.

What do you call Him? You may call Him God. You may call Him Father. Whatever you choose to call Him, God loves hearing from you.

PRAYER

Dear God, You have many great names that I can call You. Your name is so great. In Jesus' name, amen.

24

You are all children of God through faith in Christ Jesus.
—Galatians 3:26

God's Family

Some families are big,
and some families are small.
Some families have lots of kids,
and some have just one or two.
Grandpas and grandmas are
part of a family too.
Did you know that God has a family?
If you believe in Jesus, you are a
part of God's family.
God is your Father, and you
are His child.
It's wonderful to be in
God's family!

TODAY'S WORD

families

PRAYER
Dear God, I am glad that You are my
Father and that I can be in Your family.
In Jesus' name, amen.

Being with you will fill me with joy. —Psalm 16:11

Joy, Joy, Joy

"I have the joy, joy, joy, joy
down in my heart."
Kids feel happy when they sing
that song.
Do you know where joy comes from?
It comes from knowing Jesus.
If you have Jesus in your heart,
joy will be there too.
If you have joy in your heart,
you will feel happy inside.
Jesus will put joy in your heart
and a smile on your face.

PRAYER

Dear Jesus, thank You for the
joy, joy, joy You put in my heart.
In Jesus' name, amen.

For God bought you with a high price. —1 Corinthians 6:20 NLT

A High Price

When you buy something at the store,
it has a price on it.
Some things have a high price.
Some things have a low price.
Things with great value have a
high price.
When Jesus died on the cross,
He paid the price for sin.
It was a high price to pay.
But you have great value.
And God thinks you are worth it.

TODAY'S WORD

price

PRAYER

Dear Jesus, thank You for paying the price for
my sin on the cross. I am glad You think I have
great value. In Jesus' name, amen.

Be still, and know that I am God. —Psalm 46:10 NLT

Be Still

Sometimes you have to be still
in order to listen to something.
Have you ever listened to the
birds singing?
Have you ever listened to raindrops
tapping on your window?
God made the birds that sing.
God makes the rain that taps
on your window.
When we hear those sounds,
we know that God is near us.

PRAYER

Dear God, I know that You are near. Please help
me to be still so I can listen to You. In Jesus'
name, amen.

"Put God's kingdom first. Do what he wants you to do." —Matthew 6:33 NIrV

Put God First

Kids like to be the first one
in line at recess.
They like to be the first one
chosen for a team.
The Bible tells us about something
else that should be first.
We should always put God first.
He wants to be the first one
we think about every day.
When you put God first,
He will take care of
everything else.

TODAY'S WORD
first

PRAYER
Dear God, help me to put You first the way You
want me to. In Jesus' name, amen.

"You must not misuse the name of the LORD your God." —Exodus 20:7 NLT

Respect God's Name

God is holy.
It is important to show respect
to God.
We should respect God's name.
We respect God's name when
we pray to Him.
We respect His name when we talk
about how great He is.
We respect God's name when we tell
others about His love.
We respect God's name when we sing
praises to Him.
People who love God should always
respect His name.

PRAYER

Dear God, I know that You are holy. I want to respect Your name. In Jesus' name, amen.

Open my eyes to see the wonderful things in your teachings.
—Psalm 119:18

The Best Book

You can read books about
faraway places.
You can read books about
animals or people.
Do you know the very best
book you can read?
It's the Bible.
God uses the Bible to tell you
how much He loves you!
You will learn many things
when you read the Bible.
It is the best book in the world!

TODAY'S WORD

read

PRAYER

Dear God, please help me to read my
Bible and learn all about You. In Jesus'
name, amen.

BIBLE VERSE

Think about the ant! Consider its ways and be wise. —Proverbs 6:6 NIrV

Army Ants

TODAY'S WORD

work

Army ants are hard workers.
They are also strong.
They can carry food that weighs
ten times more than they do!
When army ants work together,
they can do many things.
God wants us to work together too.
You can help your brother or sister
put his or her toys away.
You can help your friend
make a snack.
You can work as a team, just like
army ants.

PRAYER

Dear Lord, please help
me to work hard and be
a good helper. In Jesus'
name, amen.

I praise God for his word to me. I praise the LORD for his word.
—Psalm 56:10

Important Words

The Bible is the Word of God.
All of the words in the Bible are
from God.
He told the writers what to say.
The Word of God is how God
talks to us.
When we read His Word, we will
learn about God's love for us.
We will learn how to obey Him.
The words in the Bible are the
most important words in the
whole world.

TODAY'S WORD

word

PRAYER

Dear God, thank You for Your Word. Help me to
learn about You when I read Your important
words. In Jesus' name, amen.

He sent the east wind from heaven. He led the south wind by his power. —Psalm 78:26

A Windy Day

We cannot see the wind,
but we can see what it does.
Wind can blow the leaves on a tree.
Wind can blow a sailboat
across a lake.
It can even blow your hat off!
We cannot see God either,
but we can see what He does.
God moves the sun across
the sky.
He can make it rain
or snow.
And only God can make
the wind blow.

PRAYER
Dear God, I look all around and I can see the things You do. Help me to see You every day. In Jesus' name, amen.

The LORD Most High is wonderful. He is the great King over all the earth. —Psalm 47:2

How Wonderful

It is wonderful to hold a puppy.
It is wonderful when Grandma
comes for a visit.
When something is wonderful,
it is good or great.
Wonderful things make us happy.
The Bible says that God is wonderful.
He is good and great.
There is nothing more wonderful
than God and His love for us.
Isn't that wonderful?

TODAY'S WORD

wonderful

PRAYER

Dear God, You are so wonderful! Thank You for
Your wonderful love. In Jesus' name, amen.

A Free Gift

TODAY'S WORD

free

Kids like getting free gifts.
So do grown-ups!
The Bible tells us about the best
gift we can get.
And it is free!
When we believe in Jesus, our free
gift is a happy life in heaven.
We can live with Jesus forever!
There is nothing to buy.
All you have to do is ask Jesus
to be your Savior.
Jesus wants you to have His
free gift.

PRAYER

Dear Jesus, thank You for Your free gift. I am happy I can live with You forever. In Jesus' name, amen.

Give thanks whatever happens. That is what God wants for you in Christ Jesus. —1 Thessalonians 5:18

Always Be Thankful

Are you thankful when you get a new toy?
Are you thankful when you eat good food?
Those are times when it's easy to be thankful.
But what if you get gum stuck on your shoe?
God wants us to be thankful no matter what.
He is always with us.
And that is something to be thankful about!

TODAY'S WORD

thankful

PRAYER
Dear God, please help me to be thankful today no matter what happens. In Jesus' name, amen.

BIBLE VERSE

I lie down and sleep. I wake up again, because the LORD *takes care of me.*
—Psalm 3:5 NIrV

God Cares for You

TODAY'S WORD

care

Do you feed the squirrels?
Do you walk your dog?
Do you give your goldfish
clean water?
Caring for animals can be fun.
Did you know God takes care of you?
He makes sure you have clothes
to wear and food to eat.
God loves taking care of you
every day.
Remember to thank God for
His care.

PRAYER

Dear God, I am thankful You take such good care
of me! In Jesus' name, amen.

Young people, enjoy yourselves while you are young. —Ecclesiastes 11:9

Enjoy Yourself

Do you like to swim
or play baseball?
Do you like to eat ice cream?
Do you like to watch a sunset
or go fishing?
There are lots of good things that
you can enjoy every day.
Did you know that God wants you
to enjoy many things?
Everything He created is for you
to enjoy.
So have a good day
and enjoy yourself!

TODAY'S WORD

enjoy

PRAYER

Dear God, thank You that You give me
so many things to enjoy. Help me to
have a good day today. In Jesus'
name, amen.

I love those who love me. Those who want me find me. —Proverbs 8:17

Hide-and-Seek

Do you like to play hide-and-seek?
It is fun to find people
who are hiding.
Did you know you can always
find God?
You can't see His face,
but you can see the things
He has made.
God made the sky and the ocean.
He made the moon and stars.
And He makes pretty sunsets.
Just look for God,
and you will find Him.

PRAYER
Dear God. I am happy that I can always find You.
Help me to see You today. In Jesus' name, amen.

We know that in everything God works for the good of those who love him. —Romans 8:28

It's All Good

Do you like making new friends?
Are you happy when you
get a good grade in school?
Do you like going on a trip?
It's nice when good things happen.
The Bible says that God can make
everything turn out to be good.
It might not happen right away,
but keep loving God.
He will make everything good.

TODAY'S WORD
good

PRAYER

Dear God. I know that
You can make all things
good. Help me to always
remember that. In
Jesus' name. amen.

Depend on God

TODAY'S WORD

depend

Can you count to 10?
Can you count to 50?
Can you count to 100?
Did you know that you can
count on God?
To count on God means
to depend on Him.
He knows everything, all the time.
You can always depend on God
and the Bible to give you answers.
Isn't it great you have a God
you can depend on?

PRAYER

Dear God, thank You for always being there for me. I am happy I can depend on You! In Jesus' name, amen.

I praise you because you made me in an amazing and wonderful way.
—Psalm 139:14

You Are Amazing

Can you jump up and down?

Can you wiggle your nose?

Can you tie your shoe?

Can you read a book?

What else can you do?

God made you just the way you are.

God made you so that you can do

many wonderful things.

You are a special part

of God's creation.

Praise God because you are amazing!

PRAYER

Dear God. I praise You for making me the way I am. Thank You that I can do so many things. In Jesus' name, amen.

BIBLE VERSE

He named the water that was gathered together "seas." God saw that this was good. —Genesis 1:10

We Need Water

TODAY'S WORD
water

People need water to drink.
Animals need water too.
The grass needs water.
Trees and flowers need water.
Do you know where water comes from?
God created water when He made
the rivers and lakes.
God makes it rain when the earth
is dry.
Water is important.
God knows we need water.
That's why He created it.

PRAYER

Dear God, thank You that You made water. You always know what we need. In Jesus' name, amen.

He has put his angels in charge of you. They will watch over you wherever you go. —Psalm 91:11

Watching over You

God sends His angels to watch over us.

Angels watch over you when you go to school or to your friend's house.

They watch over you when you play soccer or ride your bike.

They watch over you when you eat and when you sleep.

God sends His angels to be with you all the time.

That's because He loves you.

PRAYER

Dear God, thank You for angels who watch over me and keep me safe. In Jesus' name, amen.

"You are my friends if you do what I command you." —John 15:14

Good Friends

Good friends are fun to play with.
Good friends are nice to talk to.
Good friends help each other out.
Did you know Jesus wants to be
your friend too?

If you love Jesus, He will be
your friend.

You can talk to Him.
He will help you out.
It's good to have good friends.
But Jesus is the best friend
you can have!

PRAYER

Dear Jesus, thank You for being my
friend. Help me to be a good friend
to others. In Jesus' name, amen.

God loves the person who gives happily. —2 Corinthians 9:7

Giving Happily

Getting gifts is fun!

Giving gifts is fun too.

What are some things you can give?

You can give a hug to your mom.

You can give a toy to your brother
or sister.

You can give some clothes to
people who need them.

There are so many things
you can give.

Just remember to give with a
big smile on your face.

TODAY'S WORD

give

PRAYER

Dear Lord, thank You for all that You give me. Help
me to be happy when I give to others. In Jesus'
name, amen.

"I am putting my rainbow in the clouds." —Genesis 9:13

Pretty Colors

Do you have a favorite color?
Is it blue like the sky?
Is it yellow like the sun?
Is it pink like a flower?
Is it green like a frog on a
lily pad?
Do you think God has
a favorite color?
God made many colors for us to see.
He even paints the sky with
colorful sunsets and rainbows.
Enjoy all the pretty colors
God created for you!

PRAYER

Dear God, thank You for all the pretty colors. Help me see the beauty in what You have created. In Jesus' name, amen.

Millions and Millions

Have you ever tried to count
the stars?
Can you guess how many there are?
Even the smartest person doesn't
know how many stars there are.
Scientists know there are millions
and millions of stars.
But they cannot count them all.
Only God can count all the stars.
And He gives a name to every star.
That's a lot of names!

TODAY'S WORD

millions

PRAYER

Dear God, when I look at the stars, I think about
how great You are. In Jesus' name, amen.

You are young, but do not let anyone treat you as if you were not important. —1 Timothy 4:12

You Are Important

Kings and rulers are important.
Doctors and nurses are important.
Moms and dads are important.
Teachers are important too.
Can you think of other people who
are important?
You don't have to be a grown-up
to be important.
You are important to God.
You are His child and He loves you.
Before you go to bed tonight,
say to yourself, "I am important
because God loves me!"

PRAYER

Dear God, thank You that I am important to You. Help me to always remember that. In Jesus' name, amen.

God will yet fill your mouth with laughter. —Job 8:21

A Good Joke

Jokes can make you laugh.
They can make you happy.
God wants us to laugh and be happy.
What kind of jokes should you tell?
You should always tell good jokes.
They can even be silly.
When you tell a good joke,
you can make your friends laugh.
Then you can all laugh and be
happy together!

TODAY'S WORD

joke

PRAYER
Dear Lord, thank You for fun and laughter. Thank You for happy times. In Jesus' name, amen.

God Never Changes

TODAY'S WORD

change

Do you have a picture of when you were a baby?
Have you changed a lot since that picture?
Babies don't stay babies very long.
And kids grow up to be adults.
People change as they get older.
But God never changes.
God's love never changes either.
God will always stay the same forever and ever!

PRAYER

Dear God, thank You that You will never change and that You will always love me. In Jesus' name, amen.

God has given us different gifts for doing certain things well.
—Romans 12:6 NLT

Good at Something

TODAY'S WORD

certain

Some kids are good at running.

Some kids are good at singing.

Some kids are good at reading.

Some kids are good at drawing pictures.

God made us so we can do

certain things well.

Maybe you are good at making

friends or helping others.

Whatever you are good at,

thank God for making you

that way.

PRAYER

Dear God, thank You that I can be good at certain things. I know You made me just the way I am. In Jesus' name, amen.

Lots of Comfort

TODAY'S WORD

comfort

Do you like to hug your mom?
Do you like to curl up in a soft
blanket when you are sleepy?
Do you like a cup of hot cocoa
when you are chilly?
These things can give you comfort
and make you feel good inside.

God can give you comfort too.
When you talk to Him, He will
make you feel good inside.

PRAYER

Dear God, thank You that You give
me comfort. In Jesus' name,
amen.

Happy are the people who know how to praise you. —Psalm 89:15

Praise God

Are you happy when you
get a special treat?
Are you happy when you
can play outside?
The Bible tells us how we can be happy.
People who praise God are happy.
When you praise God, you tell Him
how great and wonderful He is.
You can praise God by telling Him
that you love Him.
Go ahead and try it!
Praise God and be happy.

TODAY'S WORD

praise

PRAYER

Dear God. You are great and wonderful. I love
You because You love me. In Jesus' name, amen.

A Special Helper

When you ask Jesus into your heart,
God gives you a special helper.
This helper is the Holy Spirit.
You can't see the Holy Spirit,
but He lives inside of you.
He helps you to know what is right.
He helps you to make good choices.
All you have to do is ask for help.
It's great to have a helper
with you all the time!

PRAYER

Dear God, thank You for sending the Holy Spirit
to be my helper. In Jesus' name, amen.

I pray that you will be active in sharing what you believe.
—Philemon v.6 NIrV

The Best Thing to Share

TODAY'S WORD
share

You can share a cookie with
your mom or dad.
You can share your crayons with your
brother or sister.
Do you know what else you can share?
You can share your Bible storybook
with a friend.
You can share about Jesus and
how much He loves you.
Remember to share about Jesus.
That is the best thing you can
share with anyone!

PRAYER
Dear Jesus, help me to share
about You with everyone
I know. In Jesus' name,
amen.

BIBLE VERSE

Shout with joy to the Lord, all the earth. Burst into songs and praise.
—Psalm 98:4

Music to His Ears

TODAY'S WORD

music

People sing songs to God.
People dance to music for God.
Do you like to sing or play drums?
God loves to hear music when we
worship Him.

You can even make up your own songs
to praise Him!
Dance around and tell God
how much you love Him.
Play the drums and shout to God.
He loves to hear your music!

PRAYER

Dear God, I am glad
You like to hear my
songs. Help me to
worship You. In
Jesus' name, amen.

My God is my rock. I can run to him for safety. —Psalm 18:2

God Is Our Rock

Lizards like to hide under rocks.
Rocks can keep lizards cool when
it is hot outside.
Rocks can keep lizards safe from
other animals.
Rocks are strong.
They don't crumble or fall apart.
The Bible says that God is our rock.
God is strong and powerful.
You can ask Him to help you.
He wants to keep you safe,
just like a rock.

TODAY'S WORD

rock

PRAYER

God, You are my rock. Please keep me safe.
Thank You for Your love. In Jesus' name, amen.

Ruler of All

Some countries have a president
who rules over the people.
Other countries have a king.
Rulers are supposed to take care
of the people in their country.
Did you know that Jesus is a ruler?
He doesn't just rule a country.
He rules the whole world.
Jesus is the Ruler over all the
other rulers.
He takes care of His people.

PRAYER

Dear Jesus, You are my Ruler and my King.
Thank You for caring for Your people. In Jesus'
name, amen.

True Stories

Stories are fun to read.
Some stories are true.
But some stories are not true.
The Bible has many good stories
to read.
Do you know the story of Noah
and the ark?
Have you read about Jonah
and the whale?
Those stories were written
a long time ago.
God told the writers what to write.
That's how we know they are true.

TODAY'S WORD

true

PRAYER

Dear God, thank You for giving me
so many true stories to read in
the Bible. In Jesus' name, amen.

The LORD longs to show you his favor. He wants to give you his tender love.
—Isaiah 30:18 NIrV

Favorite Things

TODAY'S WORD

favorite

What is your favorite song?
What is your favorite animal?
What is your favorite food?
When something is your favorite,
that means you like it a lot.
Everyone has favorite things.
Did you know God has favorite
things too?
You are His child.
You are one of His favorite things.
That means He likes you a lot!

PRAYER

Dear God, thank You that I am one of
Your favorite things. I am happy that You
love me so much. In Jesus' name, amen.

"Love the Lord your God. Love him with all your heart, all your soul, all your mind, and all your strength." —Mark 12:30

You Decide

Do you decide what books to read?
Do you decide what toys to
play with?
Sometimes kids get to decide
certain things.
But sometimes parents help kids
make decisions.
There is something you can decide
by yourself.
You can decide to love God.
You can love Him with all of your
heart and soul and mind and strength.
It's the best decision you can make.

TODAY'S WORD

decide

PRAYER

Dear God, I want to love You the best that I can.
Help me to love You more every day. In Jesus'
name, amen.

Call on God

TODAY'S WORD

call

Do you like making phone calls?
Do you call your grandma?
Do you call your friends to wish
them a happy birthday?
Have you ever called God?
You don't need a phone
to call Him.
All you have to do is talk to God
and He hears you.
The next time you want to
make a call,
you can call God.
He is never too busy to answer.

Hi, God!

PRAYER

Dear God, thank You that I can call on You anytime.
I love talking to You. In Jesus' name, amen.

God will have a house for us to live in. . . . It will be a home in heaven that will last forever. –2 Corinthians 5:1

A House for You

Did you know God has a house
for you in heaven?
The houses in heaven are beautiful.
The streets are made of gold.
There are pretty stones all around.
It is always happy and bright.
You don't have to go there now.
But someday you can live with God
in heaven forever.
He will welcome you to your
new home.
And it will be beautiful!

TODAY'S WORD

house

PRAYER

Dear God, thank You that someday
I will live in a beautiful house in
heaven. In Jesus' name, amen.

So God made the wild animals, the tame animals and all the small crawling animals. —Genesis 1:25

God's Animals

TODAY'S WORD

animals

Have you ever been to the zoo?
What kinds of animals did you see?
God made many different animals
when He created the world.
He made big elephants.
He made tiny mice.
He made monkeys and bears
and tigers too.
What is your favorite animal
that God made?
God made the animals.
Then He made us to take care
of them.
Animals are a
part of God's
wonderful creation.

PRAYER
Dear God, thank You for making all of the animals
for me to enjoy! In Jesus' name, amen.

Never stop praying. —1 Thessalonians 5:17

Say a Prayer

Do you say a prayer before you eat dinner?

Do you say a prayer before you go to bed?

There are many things you can pray about.

You can thank God for the food He gives you.

You can ask God to help you be kind to your friends.

You can say a prayer to tell God how much you love Him.

God loves hearing from you when you pray.

TODAY'S WORD

prayer

PRAYER

Dear God, thank You for always listening to me when I pray. In Jesus' name, amen.

The Lord is my shepherd. I have everything I need. —Psalm 23:1

Jesus the Shepherd

A shepherd's job is to take care of his sheep.

He feeds them and keeps them safe.

The shepherd loves his sheep.

The sheep follow the shepherd.

They know he will give them everything they need.

The Bible tells us that Jesus is our Shepherd.

We are His sheep.

If we follow Him, He will take care of us just like a shepherd takes care of his sheep.

PRAYER

Dear Jesus. You are the best Shepherd. Thank You for taking care of me. In Jesus' name. amen.

The glory of the Lord shines on you. —Isaiah 60:1

Shine Like a Penny

Have you ever held a new penny
in your hand?
People notice new pennies because
they are bright and shiny.
When you become a Christian,
the Holy Spirit lives inside you.
The Holy Spirit makes you like a
new person on the inside.
He fills you up with God's love.
Then you will shine on the outside,
just like a new penny.

PRAYER
Dear God, thank You for making me new on the inside.
I want to shine for You. In Jesus' name, amen.

69

Let us think about each other and help each other to show love and do good deeds. —Hebrews 10:24

Good Deeds

TODAY'S WORD

deed

Do you help your mom set the table?
If you do, that's a good deed.
Do you help your grandma
water her plants?
That's a good deed too.
A good deed is when you do something
nice for someone else.
Jesus wants us to do good deeds.
When we do a good deed, it shows
that we love Jesus.
What good deed can you do today?

PRAYER

Dear Jesus, thank You for all the
things You do for me.
Please help me do good
deeds for others. In
Jesus' name, amen.

"I know you by name." —Exodus 33:17 ESV

A New Name

When you were born, you were given
a name.
You were given a first name and
a last name.
Do you have a middle name too?
Some kids are named after someone
in their family.
Names are important.
They tell others who we are.
When you ask Jesus into your heart,
you get another name.
The name is Christian.
It's an important name.
It means you are in God's family.

TODAY'S WORD

name

PRAYER

Dear God, thank You that I can be a Christian and
be in Your family. In Jesus' name, amen.

A New Creature

TODAY'S WORD

creature

A caterpillar does not stay
a caterpillar.
After a while, a caterpillar turns
into a butterfly.
A butterfly is a beautiful
new creature.
The Bible says that we can become
new creatures too.
When you ask Jesus into your
heart, you become a new creature.
You still look the same
on the outside.
But Jesus makes you a beautiful
new creature on the inside.

PRAYER

Dear Jesus, I am glad that I can
be made new by asking You into
my heart. In Jesus' name, amen.

Two people are better than one. They get more done by working together.
—Ecclesiastes 4:9

Working Together

It's hard to play catch by yourself.
It's better to do it with
someone else.
Some things are made to be done together.
And some things are easier when
you do them together.
Cleaning your room by yourself
can be hard.
If someone helps you, the job
gets done faster.
Working together is God's idea.
It is good to work together
and help each other.

TODAY'S WORD

together

PRAYER

Dear God, please help me to work together with others. In Jesus' name, amen.

"People look at the outside of a person, but the LORD looks at the heart."
—1 Samuel 16:7

A Beautiful Heart

TODAY'S WORD
heart

What do you see when you look
in the mirror?
Do you see your eyes?
Do you see your nose and mouth?
Can you see your heart?
No, you cannot see your heart.
But God can.
God thinks you are beautiful.
He wants your heart to be
beautiful too.
If you love God, you
will have a
beautiful heart.
And God will see it.

PRAYER

Dear God, I want
to love You so I can
have a beautiful
heart. In Jesus'
name, amen.

LORD, you bless those who do what is right. —Psalm 5:12

Blessings from God

God gives us good things.

They are called blessings.

Food and water are blessings.

Sunshine and rain are blessings.

Flowers and trees are blessings.

Friends and family are blessings.

Good health is a blessing too.

God wants to bless us.

He blesses us because He loves us.

God gives us blessings every day.

He wants us to enjoy them.

Enjoy God's blessings

and remember to say thank You.

PRAYER

Dear God, thank You that You love me. Thank You for the blessings I enjoy every day. In Jesus' name, amen.

Every word that God speaks is true. —Proverbs 30:5 ERV

Tell the Truth

God always tells the truth.
God wants us to tell the truth too.
We need to tell the truth to our
mom and dad.
We need to tell the truth to our
teachers and friends.
Sometimes it is hard to tell
the truth.
But it's always the right thing
to do.
If you need help, just ask God
and He will help you.

PRAYER

Dear God, I know Your words are always
true. Help me to tell the truth, even when it
is hard. In Jesus' name, amen.

He changes the times and seasons of the year. —Daniel 2:21

Favorite Season

Do you like to swim in
the summer?
Do you play in the leaves
in the fall?
Do you build snowmen
in the winter?
Do you pick flowers for your mom
in the spring?
God made the seasons for you
to enjoy.
He sends the rain and the snow.
He makes the sun shine.
And He makes the flowers grow.
You can enjoy God's beautiful world
all year long.

TODAY'S WORD

season

PRAYER
Dear God, thank You for
making the seasons for
me to enjoy! In Jesus'
name, amen.

"For nothing is impossible with God." —Luke 1:37 NLT

God Can Do Anything

It is impossible for people to fly
like birds.
It is impossible for people to live
underwater with the fish.
People can do a lot of things.
But some things are impossible to do.
Did you know that God can
do anything?
The Bible says that nothing is
impossible with God.
If you need His help, just ask.
Nothing is too hard for Him.

PRAYER

Dear Lord, I know You can do anything.
I know You can always help me. Thank
You for being such a great God. In
Jesus' name, amen.

God's Path

A path in the woods might take you
to a wonderful place.
But if it goes in a circle,
you will end up where you started.
God has a path for your life.
If you love Him, He will lead
you down that path.
God's path is always the best path.
It will never go in a circle!
It will lead you to a wonderful place.

PRAYER

Dear Lord, thank You that You will always lead me down the right path. In Jesus' name, amen.

TODAY'S WORD

path

You're a Star

It's fun to go outside at night
and look at all the stars.
The stars are very far away.
But we can see the stars because
they are so bright.
The Bible says that people who
love Jesus are like stars.
When we show love to others,
the love of Jesus shines through us.
Do you love Jesus?
Do you love others?
Then you're a star!

PRAYER

Dear Jesus, help me to shine like the stars and to show love to my family and friends. In Jesus' name, amen.

He satisfies the thirsty. He fills up the hungry. —Psalm 107:9

Be Satisfied

When you are hungry, you eat food.
When you are thirsty, you get
a drink of water.
Eating and drinking make you
feel satisfied.
Did you know you can be hungry
and thirsty for God?
When you want to learn about God,
it's like being hungry and thirsty.
The Bible is food and drink
for your soul.
Reading the Bible and learning
more about God will make you
feel satisfied.

TODAY'S WORD

satisfied

PRAYER

Dear God, thank You that I can learn more about You from the Bible. I want to be satisfied. In Jesus' name, amen.

Pleasant words are like honey. They are sweet to the spirit and bring healing to the body. —Proverbs 16:24 NIrV

Sweet Words

TODAY'S WORD

sweet

Honey is sweet.
Putting honey on your food
makes your food taste sweet.
Did you know words can be sweet too?
Please and *thank you* are sweet words.
You can use sweet words to say,
"I love you."
You can use sweet words to pray
for someone who is sick.
Sweet words make people happy.
When you say sweet words, it's like
having honey on your tongue.

PRAYER
Dear God, please help me to use
sweet words every day. In Jesus'
name, amen.

The Lord is close to everyone who prays to him. —Psalm 145:18

God Is Close

The world is very big.
The world has many people
who live in it.
There are many different countries
and many different languages.
We do not understand all the
different languages.
But God does.
God listens to anyone who prays to
Him no matter what language
they speak.
And even though the world is big,
God can be close to everyone
at the same time.

TODAY'S WORD

world

PRAYER
Dear God, thank You that You are close
to me whenever I pray. In Jesus'
name, amen.

Your Wonderful Body

masterpiece

Do you like to play baseball?
God gave you legs so you can
run around the bases.
Do you like to color pictures?
God gave you hands so you can
color a masterpiece.
Do you like to sing?
God gave you a voice so you
can sing happy songs.
God made our bodies so we can
do wonderful things.
You are His masterpiece.

PRAYER

Dear God, thank You that I am Your masterpiece.
I am thankful for all the things I can do. In
Jesus' name, amen.

What Will You Be?

What do you want to be
when you grow up?
Do you want to be a fire fighter?
Do you want to be a doctor who
takes care of animals?
God knows what you will be.
He has it all planned.
He wants the very best for you.
Remember to ask Him what He
wants you to be.
You can be anything if that
is what God wants for you.

TODAY'S WORD

want

PRAYER

Dear God, please help me
to know what You want
me to be. In Jesus'
name, amen.

Tick, Tock

TODAY'S WORD

time

Do you spend time playing
with your friends?
Do you spend time reading books?
Do you spend time eating a
good meal?
Did you know God wants you to
spend time with Him too?
You can spend time with God
by reading your Bible.
You can talk to God and
say a prayer.
God loves it when you spend
time together.

PRAYER

Dear God, help me to make time for important things, like spending time with You. In Jesus' name, amen.

"But I will make you healthy again. I will heal your wounds."
—Jeremiah 30:17 NIrV

God Heals Us

Have you ever skinned your knee?
Did your mom give it a kiss
and put a bandage on it?
Skinned knees get better.
That's the way God made our bodies.
God heals skinned knees.
He heals runny noses and even
broken bones.
Bumps and hurts don't last long.
God will heal you.
Then you can run and play with
your friends.

TODAY'S WORD

heal

PRAYER
Dear Lord, thank You
that You can heal me
when I am hurt. In
Jesus' name, amen.

The Best Secret-Keeper

secret

Have you ever told a secret
to a friend?
Did a friend ever tell you a secret?
When you tell someone a secret,
you don't want other people
to know about it.
Sometimes it is hard for
people to keep secrets.
But it is not hard for God.
God will always keep our secrets.
We can tell Him anything,
and He will not tell!

PRAYER

Dear Jesus, thank You that I can trust You to keep my secrets. In Jesus' name, amen.

He is Lord of lords and King of kings. —Revelation 17:14

King of All

Lions are strong and powerful.
They rule over all the other animals.
That is why they are called
the king of the jungle.
Some countries have kings who
rule over the people.
You have a King too.
Do you know who your King is?
God is your King.
He is the most powerful
King of all.
He is King over everything,
even the lions!

TODAY'S WORD

king

PRAYER

Dear God, You are the best King of all. Thank You for being my King. In Jesus' name, amen.

Way to Go

TODAY'S WORD

cheer

Way to go!
Great job!
It's nice to hear those words
when someone cheers for you.
It makes you feel good inside.
When you cheer for others,
it makes them feel good too.
You can tell your friends they did
a great job at the spelling bee.
You can tell your mom you
like the dinner she made.
God wants us to cheer
for one another.
It makes everyone
happy.

PRAYER

Dear God, help me to cheer
for others the way You want
me to. In Jesus' name, amen.

Everything that God made is good. —1 Timothy 4:4

Good to Be Different

Do rabbits have fins?

Do fish have feet?

Of course not!

God made them different from
each other.

Rabbits have feet so they can hop.

Fish have fins so they can swim.

God made people to be different too.

Your friends may be short or tall.

They may have brown hair
or blond hair.

You are different from your friends.

It's good to be different.

And God loves us all.

TODAY'S WORD
different

PRAYER

Dear God, thank You for making all of us
different. I am thankful that I am one of a kind!
In Jesus' name, amen.

If God is for us, who can be against us. —Romans 8:31 NIV

On Your Team

TODAY'S WORD

team

Do you like to play games like
soccer or baseball?
It's fun to be on a team.
And it's always fun to be
on a good team!
Good teammates help us
to play better.
They help us to be strong
against the other team.
Did you know that God is
on your team?
Even when you're not playing a game,
He will help you to do your best.

PRAYER

Dear God, thank You for always being on my
team! In Jesus' name, amen.

The earth and everything in it belong to the Lord. The world and all its people belong to him. —Psalm 24:1

Everything Is His

You can see many things when
you go for a walk.
You can see trees and flowers.
You can see the sun shining
in the sky.
You might see birds looking for
worms or squirrels eating acorns.
You might see other kids going
for a walk too.
Did you know that everything
you see belongs to God?
God made everything.
That's why it all belongs to Him.

TODAY'S WORD

everything

PRAYER

Dear God, thank You for making everything. I am glad it all belongs to You. In Jesus' name, amen.

Come Near to God

When you sit next to someone,
you are near them.
Even though you can't see God,
you can be near to Him too.
You can come near to God
by talking to Him.
You can come near to God
by reading the Bible.
You can come near to God
by singing songs about Him.
When you come near to God,
it's like sitting next to Him.

PRAYER

Dear God, thank You that I can come near to You
every day. In Jesus' name, amen.

"I am the Lord. There is no other God. I am the only God." —Isaiah 45:5

Only One Lord

Lord is another name for God.
The word *Lord* means "king"
or "master."
God is our Lord.
He is our King and Master.
God was here before the world began.
He will be here forever.
There is only one Lord.
He is your God in heaven.
He is the one who watches over you.
He is the one who answers
your prayers.
Thank Him today for being your Lord.

TODAY'S WORD

Lord

PRAYER

Dear God, You are the
only God. Thank You
for being my Lord. In
Jesus' name, amen.

Finish It

It takes time to build a good fort.
First you start at the bottom.
Then you add the sides.
Then you put on the top
to finish it.
God builds good things too,
and you are one of them.
He started working on you
before you were born.
He wants to do good things
through you.
God will keep working on you
until He is finished.

PRAYER
Dear God, thank You for working in me to do something good. In Jesus' name, amen.

I thank God every time I remember you. —Philippians 1:3

Remember Them

Do you have a friend or relative
who lives far away?
Do they come to visit you?
Do you think about them after
they leave?
When you think about them, you can
remember the fun you had together.
You can look forward to seeing
them again.
When you think about them,
remember to thank God for them.
Even though they live far away,
you can pray for them every day.

PRAYER

Dear God, thank You for the people I love no
matter where they live. Please watch over them.
In Jesus' name, amen.

So Much Love

Moms and dads give gifts to their children because they love them so much.

God gives gifts to His children too.

God loves you so much that He gave you His Son, Jesus.

Jesus is our Savior.

Jesus will forgive your sins.

Whoever believes in Jesus will live with God forever.

Jesus is the best gift you can get.

Remember to thank God for loving you so much.

PRAYER

Dear God, thank You for loving me so much. Thank You for Jesus, my Savior. In Jesus' name, amen.

Let the Children Come

TODAY'S WORD

children

When Jesus lived on the earth,
people followed Him.
Some of the people were old,
and some were young.
Jesus wanted to be with everyone.
He told the children to come to Him.
He wanted to talk to them
and bless them.
Jesus still loves children today.
He loves you and wants to
bless you.
You can talk to Jesus
when you pray.
He wants you to come
to Him.

PRAYER

Dear Jesus, thank You that
You love children so much.
I want to come to You. In
Jesus' name, amen.

BIBLE VERSE

Children, obey your parents in all things. This pleases the Lord.
—Colossians 3:20

Try to Please God

TODAY'S WORD

please

Do you know what it means to
please God?
It means to make Him happy.
We please God when we are kind
to our friends.
We please God when we help
our brother or sister.
We please God when we tell
the truth.
We please God when we obey
our parents.
We please God when we say
thank you.
There are many ways that you can
please God today.

PRAYER

Dear God, help me to
please You today. In
Jesus' name, amen.

BIBLE VERSE

Good news makes you feel better. Your happiness will show in your eyes.
—Proverbs 15:30

Good News

People like hearing good news.
Good news makes them happy.
The birth of a new baby
is good news.
Getting a good grade on a test
is good news.
When a sick person gets better,
it is good news.
The best news is that Jesus
loves you.
Jesus forgives your sins.
Jesus gives you eternal life.
Good news like that should make
you smile and be happy!

TODAY'S WORD

news

PRAYER

Dear God, thank You for the good news of
Jesus. In Jesus' name, amen.

When Jesus finished saying these things, the people were amazed at his teaching. —Matthew 7:28

A Great Teacher

TODAY'S WORD
teacher

Teachers help us learn many things.
They teach us what we need to know.
The greatest Teacher is Jesus.
When Jesus lived on the earth,
He taught people about God.
He taught them how to love each
 other and how to love God.
 The things He taught are in
 the Bible.
 We can learn from Him when we
read His words.
 Jesus can be your Teacher too.

PRAYER

Dear Jesus. You are a great Teacher. Please teach me what I need to learn. In Jesus' name, amen.

Be Glad

Are you glad when it is
your birthday?
Are you glad when you can have
a party with cake and ice cream?
Are you glad when you get to
open presents?
Birthdays are fun.
They can make us glad.
The Bible says we can always be
glad in the Lord.
That way you can be glad every day,
even if it's not your birthday.

TODAY'S WORD

glad

PRAYER

Dear God, thank
You that I can be
glad in You every
day. In Jesus'
name, amen.

BIBLE VERSE

Wisdom will help you be a good person. It will help you do what is right.
—Proverbs 2:20

Get Wisdom

TODAY'S WORD

wisdom

Wise people have wisdom.
They know what is right.
They know what is wrong.
Wisdom helps a person to make
good choices.
You can get wisdom from your
parents and grandparents.
You can get wisdom from your
Sunday school teacher.
And you can get wisdom from
reading the Bible.

God wants you to have wisdom.
It will help you do what is right.

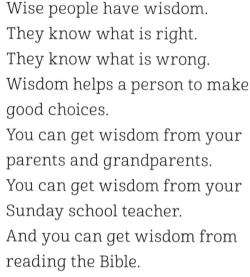

PRAYER

Dear God, please help me to have
wisdom so I can do what is right. In
Jesus' name, amen.

[Jesus] looked up to heaven and thanked God for the bread.
—Mark 6:41

A Good Example

One day Jesus fed a big crowd
of people.
He had only five loaves of bread
and two fish.
But Jesus fed all the people.
Do you know what Jesus did
before He fed the people?
He prayed and thanked God
for the food.
Jesus is our example.
We need to be more like Him.
You can follow Jesus' example.
Before you eat, remember to
thank God for your food.

TODAY'S WORD

example

PRAYER

Dear Jesus, please help me to follow Your
example. Help me to remember to thank God for
my food. In Jesus' name, amen.

Trust God

God wants you to trust Him.
He wants you to believe in Him.
You can trust that God will take
care of you.
You can trust that He will give you
what you need.
You can trust that He will always
love you.
When you trust God, you don't have
to worry.
When you trust God, you can be happy.

PRAYER

Dear God, thank You that I can trust You. I know
I can be happy and not worry because You love
me. In Jesus' name, amen.

I can do all things through Christ because he gives me strength.
—Philippians 4:13

Be Strong

Some people are very strong.
They can lift heavy boxes.
Did you know that Jesus makes
us strong?
The strength He gives is not
for lifting boxes.
Jesus helps us to be strong on the
inside so we can do what is right.
He helps us to be strong so we
won't be afraid.
Do you want to be strong
like that?
Ask Jesus to give
you strength,
and He will.

TODAY'S WORD

strong

PRAYER

Dear Jesus, please help
me to be strong. I want
to get my strength
from You. In Jesus'
name, amen.

Have Faith

TODAY'S WORD
faith

We cannot see the stars during
the day, but we know they are there.
We cannot see the air,
but we know it is real.
When you believe in something
you cannot see, it is called faith.
We cannot see God,
but we know He is real.
We cannot see Him,
but He is everywhere.
If you believe God is real,
then you have faith.

PRAYER
Dear God. I know You are real. I have faith in
You. In Jesus' name. amen.

Noah did everything that God commanded him. —Genesis 6:22

Noah Obeyed

God told Noah to build a big boat
called an ark.
Noah obeyed and did everything
God told him to do.
People laughed at Noah.
But Noah obeyed anyway.
Soon the rain came.
Noah and his family were safe inside
the boat because they obeyed.
God wants us to obey Him
no matter what others think.
Obey God, and He will take
care of you.

TODAY'S WORD
Noah

PRAYER
Dear God, please
help me to obey You
just like Noah did. In
Jesus' name, amen.

God's Grace

TODAY'S WORD

grace

Do you know someone whose
name is Grace?
Grace is a name,
but it is also a word.
The Bible talks about God's grace.
Grace is the love and kindness
God shows to us.
When God forgives our sins,
it's because of His grace.
When Jesus died on the cross for us,
it was because of God's grace.
God's grace is a gift to us.
It's a gift of love.

PRAYER

Dear God, thank You for Your gift of grace.
In Jesus' name, amen.

Let everything that breathes praise the Lord. —Psalm 150:6

Praise the Lord

People need to breathe.
Animals need to breathe.
Even plants and flowers need
to breathe.
God is the one who gives life.
God is the one who created us
to breathe.
That is why every living thing
can praise God.
Birds praise God with their songs.
Flowers praise God with their beauty.
People praise God with their prayers.
Can you breathe?
Then you can praise God.

TODAY'S WORD
breathe

PRAYER
Lord, I praise You for
giving me life. I praise
You for being so great.
In Jesus' name, amen.

Open Your Eyes

TODAY'S WORD

eyes

If you want to read a book, you need to open your eyes.

You can learn many great things from reading a book.

You can learn about whales and tigers.

You can learn about spaceships and planets.

The Bible is God's book.

You can learn about God's love in His book.

Before you read the Bible, ask God to show you wonderful things.

PRAYER

Dear God, help me to learn wonderful things about You when I read my Bible. In Jesus' name, amen.

A person who is careful about what he says keeps himself out of trouble.
—Proverbs 21:23

Careful Words

The words you say can be kind.
The words you say can make
someone happy.
Be careful with the words you say.
Always use kind words instead of
hurtful words.
Use words that are pleasing to God.
Use words that are pleasing to your
mom and dad.
Use words that are pleasing to
your friends.
And be sure to tell the truth.
Then your words will be
careful words.

TODAY'S WORD

careful

PRAYER
Dear God, help me to be careful
with my words so that they are pleasing
to You. In Jesus' name, amen.

You Can Believe It

TODAY'S WORD

believe

You can't believe everything
you read in a book.
Writers can make up things
that are not true.
But you can believe everything
that is in the Bible.
God told the writers what to write.
Whatever God says is true.
The Bible says that Jesus is the
Son of God.

The Bible says that Jesus loves you.
You can believe it!
It's true.

PRAYER
Dear God. I know
that everything in
the Bible is true. I
know that Jesus
loves me. In Jesus'
name. amen.

BIBLE VERSE

There are many other things that Jesus did. If every one of them were written down, I think the whole world would not be big enough for all the books that would be written. —John 21:25

Many Great Things

Jesus did many great things when
He lived on the earth.
He healed people who were sick.
He healed people who couldn't walk.
He made blind people see.
He made deaf people hear.
He even walked on water.
Many of the things Jesus did are
written in the Bible.
But Jesus did so many things that
they can't all fit into one book!

PRAYER

Dear Jesus, thank You for doing so many great things. In Jesus' name, amen.

"Look at the birds. . . . God takes care of them. And you are worth much more than birds." —Luke 12:24

Look at the Birds

TODAY'S WORD
birds

Birds can't grow their own food.
God helps them find food to eat
when they are hungry.
Flowers can't work or make clothes
for themselves.
But God helps them to grow tall
and makes them beautiful.
God takes care of the birds.
He takes care of the flowers.
You are more important than
they are.
He will take care of you too.

PRAYER
Dear God, thank You for taking care of the birds and the flowers. I know You will also take care of me. In Jesus' name, amen.

Do your best to live in peace with everyone. —Romans 12:18

Live in Peace

When people live in peace,
they do not argue or fight.
When people live in peace,
they are nice to each other.
When people live in peace,
they are happy.
God wants us to live in peace.
Sometimes it is hard.
But God wants us to do our best.
Live in peace with your friends.
Live in peace with your family.
Live in peace with everyone.

TODAY'S WORD

peace

PRAYER

Dear God, please help me to
live in peace with my friends
and family. In Jesus' name,
amen.

You are God's children whom he loves. So try to be like God.
—Ephesians 5:1

Be Like God

like

Sometimes kids try to be like
their parents.
Sometimes they try to be like
their friends.
God wants us to try to be like Him.
We can't do all the things that
God can do.
But we can be like Him in
other ways.
God loves people.
We can love people too.
God helps people.
We can help people too.
God is pleased when we try
to be like Him.

PRAYER

Dear God, please help me to
be more like You. In
Jesus' name, amen.

If one of you is having troubles, he should pray. If one of you is happy, he should sing praises. —James 5:13

No More Troubles

You can talk to God about anything.
You can thank Him for all the good
things He gives you.
You can praise Him for being
a great God.
You can also talk to God when you
have troubles.
You can tell Him how you feel.
He will help you with your troubles.
He will help you to be happy.
When you are happy, you can
sing happy songs to God.

TODAY'S WORD
troubles

PRAYER

Dear God, thank You that You care about my troubles. I know You can always help me. In Jesus' name, amen.

Who Is Jesus?

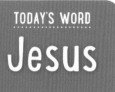

Jesus

When Jesus lived on the earth, many people followed Him. Some people thought He was a great teacher. Some people thought He was a wise man. Jesus was a great teacher. And Jesus was a wise man. But Jesus is much more than that. Jesus came down from heaven to save people from their sins. Jesus is the Son of God. He is the One who saves us.

PRAYER

Dear Jesus, thank You for coming to earth to save us. I know You are God's Son. In Jesus' name, amen.

BIBLE VERSE

The Spirit gives love, joy, peace, patience, kindness, goodness, faithfulness, gentleness, self-control. —Galatians 5:22-23

Lots of Help

When you believe in Jesus,
God gives you the Holy Spirit.
The Holy Spirit helps you to live
how God wants you to live.
The Holy Spirit helps you to love
others and be kind.
The Holy Spirit helps you to be
patient and gentle.
He gives you joy and peace.
The Holy Spirit will help you
with everything.
It's nice to have lots of help!

TODAY'S WORD

Holy Spirit

PRAYER

Dear God, thank You for the Holy Spirit. Thank You that He will help me with everything. In Jesus' name, amen.

Everywhere You Go

TODAY'S WORD

everywhere

Kids go lots of places.
They go to school.
They go to their friend's house.
They go to see their grandma.
Moms and dads do not go everywhere with their kids.
But God does.
He goes with you to school.
He goes with you to your friend's house.
He even goes to your grandma's house with you.
God goes with you everywhere.
You are never alone.

PRAYER

Dear God, thank You that You go with me everywhere I go. In Jesus' name, amen.

So let us go on to grown-up teaching. —Hebrews 6:1

Grow with God

Your body grows as you get older.
But you grow in other ways too.
When you go to school, you
grow in the things you learn.
As you get older, your knowledge
grows and grows.
God also wants you to grow in the
things you know about Him.
The more you read your Bible,
the more you will learn and grow.
Grow with God.
It's the best way
to grow!

TODAY'S WORD

grow

PRAYER
Dear God,
please help me
to grow every
day to learn more
about You. In Jesus'
name, amen.

"You are the salt of the earth." —Matthew 5:13

Pass the Salt

TODAY'S WORD
salt

People put salt on their food
to make it taste better.
Potatoes need salt.
Pretzels need salt.
Salt adds flavor to food.
Jesus wants us to be like salt.
It's not like the salt you put
on your food.
Jesus wants us to make the world
better by the way we live.
When we show His love to others,
we make it better.
The world needs that kind of salt.

PRAYER
Dear God, help me to show Your love
to others. I want the world to be full
of Your love. In Jesus' name, amen.

Work with a Smile

Sometimes you get to play.
Sometimes you have to work.
Do you ever clean your room?
Do you ever fold your clothes?
It is fun to play.
But it can also be fun to work.
When you work, you are helping others.
When you work, you are also serving God.
God wants you to do your work with a smile.
It's more fun that way.

TODAY'S WORD

smile

PRAYER
Dear God, help me to be happy when I have work to do. In Jesus' name, amen.

125

"Today in the town of David a Savior has been born to you. He is Christ the Lord." —Luke 2:11 NIrV

A Special Occasion

When a baby is born, it's a
special occasion.
The baby's parents are very happy.
They want to tell everyone about
their new baby.
On the night that Jesus was born,
an angel told the shepherds about
His birth.
The shepherds were very happy.
They ran to see baby Jesus.
Then they told everyone
that Jesus was born.
It was a very special occasion.

PRAYER

Dear Jesus, thank You for coming into the world
as a tiny baby. I know it was a very special night.
In Jesus' name, amen.

Jesus said, "I am the bread that gives life. He who comes to me will never be hungry." —John 6:35

The Best Kind of Bread

Do you like to eat bread when you
are hungry?
Does your mom buy bread
at the store?
Jesus gives us another kind
of bread.
He gives us bread for our souls.
People are hungry to know more
about Jesus.
The Bible helps us to learn all
about Him.
The Bible tells us how to be saved.
That's the kind of bread Jesus gives.

PRAYER
Dear Jesus, thank You that
I can learn more in the Bible
about the bread You give. In
Jesus' name, amen.

Clap Your Hands

People clap their hands when they are happy.
Sometimes they clap their hands when they cheer for a team.
Sometimes they clap their hands when they sing.
Did you know you can clap your hands for God?
You can shout and sing and clap to let God know you love Him.
God made your hands.
You can clap them together for Him.

PRAYER

Dear God, thank You for making my hands so I can clap them for You. In Jesus' name, amen.

128

All Day Long

In the morning, God greets us
with the rising sun.
The sun moves through the sky
all day long.
God created the sun for us.
The sun gives us light.
The sun gives us heat.
The sun helps the trees and
flowers to grow.
The sun sets at the end
of the day.
All day long God uses the sun to
bless the earth.

TODAY'S WORD

sun

PRAYER

Dear God, thank You for the sun that gives us
light and keeps us warm. In Jesus' name, amen.

Do what is right to other people. Love being kind to others. And live humbly, trusting your God. —Micah 6:8

God Tells Us

Parents tell their kids what to do
because they love them.
Sometimes they tell them how to act.
In the Bible, God tells us what to
do and how to act.
He wants us to do what is right.
He wants us to be kind to others.
He wants us to be loving.
He wants us to trust Him.
He wants us to do these things
because He loves us.

PRAYER

Dear God, I am glad the Bible tells me what You want me to do. Please help me to live that way. In Jesus' name, amen.

"Whoever can be trusted with small things can also be trusted with large things." —Luke 16:10

Small Things

Do you pick up your toys?
Do you help with the dishes?
Those may seem like small things.
But they matter.
When you learn to do small things,
it shows that you can be trusted.
When you grow up, you will have
bigger things to do.
Maybe you will drive a car
or get a job.
Whether you do big things or small
things, do your best for God.

TODAY'S WORD

small

PRAYER

Dear God, help me to do
my best in small things so
someday I can do bigger
things. In Jesus'
name, amen.

131

Be Kind

Jesus wants us to be kind.
You can be kind by sharing a snack
with your friends.
You can be kind by helping someone
who fell at recess.
You can be kind by saying please
and thank you.
You can be kind by reading a book
to someone who can't read.
Being kind to others shows that you
love Jesus.
How can you be kind to
someone today?

PRAYER

Dear Jesus, help me to be kind to others so they
will know I love You. In Jesus' name, amen.

You put him in charge of everything you made. –Psalm 8:6

You're in Charge

Do you like to be in charge?
Some kids are in charge of
feeding their pets.
Some kids are in charge of their
brother or sister while their mom
does chores.
Being in charge is important.
Did you know that God put you in charge?
He put people in charge
of His creation.
He wants us to care for the world He made.
It's an important job.

TODAY'S WORD

charge

PRAYER
Dear God, thank
You for giving us
important things
to do. Thank You
that we are in
charge of Your
creation. In
Jesus' name, amen.

Nothing in all the world can be hidden from God. —Hebrews 4:13

God Sees

TODAY'S WORD

sees

People don't always see the good things you do.

Your teacher might not know that you were kind to someone at school.

Your parents might not know that you helped your sister make her bed.

But God knows.

He sees everything you do.

He hears all the words you say.

He even knows what you are thinking.

So keep doing those good things.

God sees.

PRAYER

Dear God, I am glad that You see the good things I do. I want to do good things for You. In Jesus' name, amen.

Our Lord is great and very powerful. —Psalm 147:5

God Is Powerful

An airplane is very powerful.
A storm can be very powerful too.
But God is more powerful than
an airplane or a storm.
God can do whatever He wants to do.
He can make it rain or snow.
He can make the wind blow.
He can make the sun come up.
And He can forgive your sins.
Only God has the power to do
all of that.

PRAYER

Dear God, You are so powerful. You can do anything You want to do. Thank You for Your powerful love. In Jesus' name, amen.

"Go and make followers of all the people in the world." —Matthew 28:19

Go Tell Everyone

TODAY'S WORD

go

Jesus had a special message for His followers.
He told them to go into the world and tell others about Him.
Jesus wanted His followers to make more followers.
You can tell others about Jesus too.
You don't have to go far away.
You can tell your friends at school.
You can tell the people in your neighborhood.
Everyone needs to know about Jesus.
The world needs more Jesus followers.

PRAYER

Dear God, help me to tell others about Jesus and how much He loves us. In Jesus' name, amen.

Love One Another

Do you know where love comes from?
It comes from God.
That is why He wants us to love
each other.
He wants you to love your parents
and your grandparents.
He wants you to love your friends
and neighbors.
If you have brothers or sisters,
He wants you to love them too.
Loving others is the best way
to live.
That's because it is
God's idea.

TODAY'S WORD

love

PRAYER

Dear God, thank You
for Your love. Help
me to love others the
way You want me to.
In Jesus' name,
amen.

Pray Anyway

TODAY'S WORD

anyway

Daniel was a brave young man
who loved God.
He prayed to God three times a day.
The king made a law that people
could pray only to him!
Daniel prayed to God anyway.
Daniel was thrown into a lions' den.
But God kept Daniel safe.
You can pray wherever you are.
You don't have to pray out loud.
You can pray in your heart.
God will hear you.

PRAYER

Dear God. I know I can pray to You
anywhere. I want to be brave like Daniel.
In Jesus' name, amen.

Jesus answered, "I am the way. And I am the truth and the life. The only way to the Father is through me." —John 14:6

One Way

When people go on a trip,
they might ride in a car.
They might take a train.
They might ride on an airplane.
There are many ways for people
to travel.
But there is only one way to get
to heaven.
The Bible tells us the way.
If we want to go to heaven,
we need to ask Jesus to
forgive our sins.
He is the only way.

TODAY'S WORD

way

PRAYER
Dear Jesus, thank You
that You are the way to
heaven. In Jesus' name,
amen.

Praise the Lord for the glory of his name. Worship the Lord because he is holy. —Psalm 29:2

Worship God

TODAY'S WORD

worship

People go to church to worship God.
They sing songs and pray.
They read the Bible and listen to a
message about God.
Some people give an offering.
There are many ways to worship.
You can bow down when you worship.
You can stand tall and raise
your hands.
You can pray out loud or talk
to God quietly.
God loves it when we
worship because
it honors Him.

PRAYER
Lord, I love to
worship You. You
are great and holy.
In Jesus' name,
amen.

We do not know how to pray as we should. But the Spirit himself speaks to God for us. —Romans 8:26

Help from Above

Prayer is talking to God.
But sometimes it's hard to know
exactly what to say.
Did you know the Holy Spirit helps
us with our prayers?
He takes our words and turns them
into beautiful prayers to God.
God loves to hear you pray.
God wants you to pray from
your heart.
The Holy Spirit will make the words
exactly right.

PRAYER

Dear God, thank You that I can pray to You and that
the Holy Spirit will help me. In Jesus' name, amen.

With All Your Heart

When you do something with all your
heart, you do it completely.
You do your very best.
God wants us to love Him that way.
He wants us to praise Him that way.
He doesn't want just part of you.
He wants all of you.
Praise God with all of your heart.
When you praise God that way,
you will feel it from your
head to your toes!

PRAYER

Dear God, I will do my best to praise You with all
of my heart. In Jesus' name, amen.

You give life to everything. —Nehemiah 9:6

God Gives Life

Have you ever made a sand castle?
Have you ever made a tower
out of blocks?
It's fun for kids to create things.
Grown-ups like to create things too.
They build houses and playgrounds.
They build shopping centers
and highways.
People can create a lot of things.
But only God can create life.
God made animals and people
and trees.
Every living thing was made by God.

TODAY'S WORD

life

PRAYER

Dear God, You are
the only one who can
give life. Thank You
for giving life to me.
In Jesus' name, amen.

143

"If you have two shirts, share with the person who does not have one. If you have food, share that too." —Luke 3:11

Share with Others

Do you have clothes in your closet?

Do you have shoes to wear?

Do you have food in your kitchen?

If you have those things, be happy.

Be thankful that God gives you
what you need.

Some kids don't have enough clothes
to wear or food to eat.

If you have extra, you can share
with them.

That's what Jesus wants us to do.

PRAYER

Dear Jesus, thank You that I have clothes to wear and food to eat. Help me to share with others. In Jesus' name, amen.

Parents will tell their children what you have done. They will retell your mighty acts. —Psalm 145:4

Tell Your Children

Before the Bible was written, parents told their children all about God.

They told stories of how God led them through the sea on dry land.

They told stories of how God sent bread from heaven.

Today children learn about God from the Bible.

But parents can still tell their children about God.

If you become a parent someday, you can tell your children about God too.

TODAY'S WORD

parents

PRAYER

Dear God, thank You for the Bible and for my parents and that I can learn about You. In Jesus' name, amen.

God Keeps His Promises

God gives us many wonderful
promises in the Bible.
God promises to be with us.
God promises to take care of us.
God promises to love us.
God promises to give us
what we need.
God promises to listen when we pray.
Those are only a few promises.
There are thousands of promises
in the Bible!
And God keeps every one.

PRAYER

Dear God, thank You that You always keep Your
promises. In Jesus' name, amen.

Thanks be to God for his gift that is too wonderful to explain.
—2 Corinthians 9:15

Can't Explain It

What do you do when someone
gives you a wonderful gift?
Do you jump up and down?
Do you clap your hands?
Do you say thank you?
Sometimes it can be hard to
explain how you feel.
Jesus is the most wonderful gift
you can receive.
He loves you very much.
You don't have to explain
how you feel.
Just say thank You.

TODAY'S WORD

explain

PRAYER
Dear Jesus, thank
You for being such
a wonderful gift! In
Jesus' name, amen.

Follow the Leader

TODAY'S WORD
leader

Follow the Leader is a fun
game to play.
One person is the leader.
The other people have to do
what the leader does.
If the leader jumps,
everyone has to jump.
If the leader claps,
everyone has to clap.
Did you know Jesus is our Leader?
He wants us to follow Him.
Try to do what Jesus does.
He is the best Leader.
Follow Him.

PRAYER
Dear Jesus, thank You for being
my Leader. Help me to follow
You. In Jesus' name, amen.

You are great. You do wonderful things. You alone are God.
—Psalm 86:10 NIrV

God Is Great

Some people can win a race.

Some people can climb a mountain.

Some people can go to the moon.

Those are great things.

But only God can create the world.

Only God can make the sun shine.

Only God can make a rainbow.

Only God can make the stars

come out at night.

Only God can save us.

Those are great things that only

God can do.

TODAY'S WORD

great

PRAYER

Dear God, You are so great and wonderful. Thank You for being my God. In Jesus' name, amen.

A Special Day

TODAY'S WORD

church

Many people go to church on Sunday.
They go to praise God.
They go to learn more about God.
They go to be with other people.
Sunday is a special day to think
about God.
But you can think about God
every day of the week.
You can praise God every day.
You can read the Bible every day.
Every day is special when you think
about God.

PRAYER

Dear God, thank You that we can go to church.
Thank You that I can think about You every day.
In Jesus' name, amen.

On the seventh day God had finished his work of creation, so he rested from all his work. —Genesis 2:2 NLT

Time to Rest

Kids work hard.

They do their chores.

They go to school.

They study for tests.

You can get tired doing all of those things.

That's why God gives us time to rest.

The Bible says that God took time to rest.

He created the world in six days.

Then He rested on the seventh day.

It is good to work hard.

It is also good to rest.

PRAYER

Dear God, thank You for giving us time to rest. In Jesus' name, amen.

Jesus Makes a Promise

TODAY'S WORD

forever

Jesus gave a promise to His
followers before He went back
to heaven.
He didn't want His friends
to be sad.
He knew they would miss Him.
He told them He would be with
them forever.
They would not be able to see Him.
But He would be in their hearts.
That promise is for us too.
Jesus is in heaven.
But He is with us in our
hearts forever.

PRAYER

Dear Jesus, I am happy that You will be with me
forever. I want You to be in my heart. In Jesus'
name, amen.

I will sing to the Lord because he is worthy of great honor. —Exodus 15:1

Honor God

The Bible tells us to honor our parents.
We need to obey them and
respect them.
The Bible also says to honor God.
When we honor God, it shows God
that we love Him.
You can honor God by thanking Him
for His blessings.
You can honor God by reading
the Bible.
You can honor God by singing a
song to Him.
He is worthy of our honor.

TODAY'S WORD

honor

PRAYER
Dear God, I will honor You
because I love You. You are
worthy of my honor. In
Jesus' name, amen.

153

"I will cause food to fall like rain from the sky." —Exodus 16:4

Food from Heaven

A long time ago, God's people
were far away from home.
They were living in tents
in the desert.
They did not have any food to eat.
So God sent food from heaven.
Every morning the people went out
to pick up food from the ground.
God can send rain from heaven.
God can send snow from heaven.
And God can even send food
from heaven!

PRAYER

Dear God, thank You that
You always take care
of Your people. In
Jesus' name, amen.

Talk about them when you sit at home and walk along the road.
—Deuteronomy 6:7

Talk About Them

God gives us commandments in the
Bible because He loves us.
They teach us how to live.
They keep us happy and safe.
We can read about God's
commandments.
We can talk about them with our
friends and family.
We can talk about them at home
and at school.
Even when you go for a walk, you can
talk about God's commandments
and how much He loves you.

<table>
<tr><td>TODAY'S WORD</td></tr>
<tr><td>talk</td></tr>
</table>

PRAYER

Dear God, help me to learn about Your
commandments. I know they are good. In Jesus'
name, amen.

BIBLE VERSE

I go to bed and sleep in peace. Lord, only you keep me safe. —Psalm 4:8

God Keeps You Safe

God loves you and watches over you.
He wants to keep you safe.
You can ask Him to keep you safe
when you are at home or at school.
You can ask Him to keep you safe
when you ride your bike or go for
a walk.
And you can ask Him to keep you
safe when you go to bed.
Then you can have sweet dreams.

PRAYER
Dear Lord, please keep me safe all day
and all night. Thank You for watching
over me. In Jesus' name, amen.

He has taken our sins away from us as far as the east is from west.
—Psalm 103:12

East to West

If you travel east, you will keep going east.
If you travel west, you will keep going west.
You cannot measure how far it is from east to west.
That's how far Jesus takes our sins away.
It is too far to measure.
If we tell Jesus we are sorry for our sins, He will take our sins far away.
Then our sins will be gone forever!

TODAY'S WORD

away

PRAYER
Dear Jesus, thank You for taking my sins so far away. In Jesus' name, amen.

You received the Holy Spirit, who makes you God's child. By the Spirit's power we call God "Abba." —Romans 8:15 NIrV

Abba Father

TODAY'S WORD

Abba

Abba is a word from another language. It means "father" or "daddy." In the Bible, some people called God *Abba*. They saw God as a loving Father. God is a great King and Ruler. But He is also our Father. He loves us as His children. We can talk to God just like children talk to their fathers. He is our Abba Father.

PRAYER

Dear God, thank You that I can call You Abba Father because I am Your child. In Jesus' name, amen.

"Every animal of the forest is mine, and the cattle on a thousand hills." —Psalm 50:10 NIV

Something in Common

TODAY'S WORD

common

Cows eat grass and say moo.

Squirrels have bushy tails.

Birds have wings so they can fly.

Bunnies hop and have long ears.

Spiders make spiderwebs.

Turkeys gobble and fan out their feathers.

Raccoons like to climb trees.

Bees buzz and make honey.

Do you know what these animals

have in common?

They all belong to God!

PRAYER

Dear God, thank You for making all the animals. I know they all belong to You. In Jesus' name, amen.

BIBLE VERSE

The Lord God took dust from the ground and formed man from it. The Lord breathed the breath of life into the man's nose. —Genesis 2:7

A Special Name

TODAY'S WORD

Adam

Do you know what your name means?
Sometimes parents choose a name
for their child because of the
meaning of the name.
Did you know that God named
the first man?
God made him out of the dust
of the ground.
Then He breathed life into the man.
God named the first man Adam.
The name Adam means
"out of the earth."

PRAYER

Dear God, thank You for making people to live in the world You created. In Jesus' name, amen.

160

More and more men and women believed in the Lord and were added to the group of believers. —Acts 5:14

Many Believers

Many people followed Jesus
when He lived on the earth.
Some of the people believed that
Jesus was the Son of God.
These people were called *believers*.
After Jesus went to heaven, more and
more people became believers.
The number of believers keeps
growing and growing.
Today we have a big group
of believers called Christians.
But there is always room for more!

TODAY'S WORD

believers

PRAYER

Dear Jesus,
I am glad
that there
are so many
believers. I
want to be
a believer
too. In
Jesus' name,
amen.

The Cross of Jesus

TODAY'S WORD

cross

Do you know someone who wears a
cross around their neck?
Have you seen a cross at church?
The cross reminds us of Jesus.
Jesus died on the cross to save us.
But Jesus didn't stay on the cross.
And He didn't stay in the grave.
Jesus came back to life so we
can have eternal life.
When you see a cross, think about
how much Jesus loves you.

PRAYER

Dear Jesus, thank You for
what You did for me on the
cross. I will think about
Your love whenever I
see a cross. In Jesus'
name, amen.

With God's power working in us, God can do much, much more than anything we can ask or think of. —Ephesians 3:20

Much, Much More

People use power tools when
they work.
Power tools get the job done better.
God wants to help us do things
better too.
He gives us the Holy Spirit.
The Holy Spirit is like power
for our lives.
Whatever you have to do,
ask God to give you His power.
He will help you to do much more
than you can imagine.

TODAY'S WORD

more

PRAYER

Dear God, please give me Your power so I can do
my best at whatever I do. In Jesus' name, amen.

I am very pleased with what you have given me. I am very happy with what I've received from you. —Psalm 16:6 NIrV

Reasons to Be Happy

TODAY'S WORD

reasons

God gives you many reasons
to be happy.
He loves you very much.
He keeps you safe.
He gives you what you need.
He is always with you.
He helps you to be strong.
He will lead you and guide you.
He will help you to be wise.
And He cares about your problems.
Those are just a few reasons.
There are many more!

PRAYER

Dear God, You give me so many reasons to be happy. Thank You for blessing me so much. In Jesus' name, amen.

How can a young person live a pure life? He can do it by obeying your word.
—Psalm 119:9

A Pure Life

When the snow falls down,
it is pure and white.
It is clean and beautiful.
God wants our lives to be pure.
He wants our lives to be clean
and beautiful.
The Bible tells us how to live
pure lives.
We need to obey God's Word.
We need to ask Jesus to forgive
our sins.
Then we will be pure and clean.
Our lives will be white as snow.

TODAY'S WORD

pure

PRAYER
Dear God, please
help me to live a pure
life that is clean and
beautiful. In Jesus'
name, amen.

BIBLE VERSE

Don't ever stop being kind and truthful. Let kindness and truth show in all you do. —Proverbs 3:3

Don't Stop

TODAY'S WORD

stop

Did you ever have to stop playing
your favorite game?
Did you ever have to stop
riding your bike?
Sometimes you have to stop doing
something you enjoy because you
need to do something else.
There are some things you never have
to stop doing.
You never have to stop being kind.
You never have to stop telling
the truth.
So be kind and truthful.
Don't stop!

PRAYER

Dear Jesus, help me
to be kind and truthful
all the time. In Jesus'
name, amen.

We love because God first loved us. —1 John 4:19

Just Because

We should love the people
in our family.
We should love our friends
and neighbors.
We should love and care for
God's creation.
Do you know why?
Because that is what God
wants us to do.
Because that is the best way
to live.
And because God loved us first.
God loved you before you were born.
That's a good reason to love others!

TODAY'S WORD

because

PRAYER

Dear God, thank You for loving me even before I was born. I will love others because You love me. In Jesus' name, amen.

I will guide you and teach you the way you should go.
—Psalm 32:8 NIrV

The Best Guide

guide

Some people use a guide when they hike through the woods. That way they won't get lost. Did you know that God will be your guide?

You will face many decisions as you get older. Before you decide what to do, ask God to guide you. He will show you the best way to go. With God as your guide, you will never get lost.

PRAYER

Dear God, thank You for being my guide. Please show me where to go and what to do. In Jesus' name, amen.

Holy, holy, holy is the Lord God who rules over all.
—Revelation 4:8 NIrV

God Is Holy

God is a holy God.
That means He is perfect.
He is the King over everyone
and everything.
He is holy in all His ways.
His name is holy.
He is mighty and powerful.
He is the one and only true God.
He is the greatest of all.
The angels call Him holy.
You can call Him holy too.
When you pray, you are talking
to a holy God.

TODAY'S WORD

holy

PRAYER

Dear God. You are a holy God. You are great and mighty. Thank You that I can pray to You. In Jesus' name. amen.

"Love your neighbor as you love yourself." —Matthew 19:19

Love Your Neighbor

TODAY'S WORD

neighbor

Jesus wants us to love our neighbors.

Neighbors are people who live close to us.

But Jesus wants us to show love to other people too.

Maybe you and your parents will see someone at the store who needs help.

Maybe you will see someone on the playground who is hurt.

You can help them out and love your neighbor, even if they don't live next door.

PRAYER

Dear Jesus, please help me to love my neighbor the way You want me to. In Jesus' name, amen.

Don't be proud at all. Be completely gentle. Be patient. Put up with one another in love. —Ephesians 4:2 NIrV

Be Gentle

Have you ever held a baby?
When you hold a baby, you have
to be gentle.
You would never shout at a baby.
You need to talk softly and quietly.
God wants us to be gentle with
one another.
We should not shout at each other.
We should be tender and kind.
We should treat others with love
and respect.
You can be strong and brave
but still be gentle.

TODAY'S WORD

gentle

PRAYER
Dear God, please help me to be gentle with my friends and family. In Jesus' name, amen.

BIBLE VERSE

"You are always to remember this day. Celebrate it with a feast to the Lord."
—Exodus 12:14

A Big Meal

TODAY'S WORD

feast

A big meal is called a *feast*.
Some people have a feast at
Thanksgiving or Christmas.
In the Bible, the people had
many feasts.
They had feasts to remember how
God had taken care of them.
Many people would enjoy the
feast together.
They would say thank You to God
for all He had done for them.
When you have a feast, you can say
thank You to God too.

PRAYER

Dear God, thank You for food to eat. Thank You for taking care of me and my family. In Jesus' name, amen.

Jesus spoke all these things to the crowd by using stories.
—Matthew 13:34 NIrV

Good Stories

When Jesus was here, He talked to
big crowds of people.
He told them about God.
He told them how to love each other.
Sometimes He told stories that had
a special meaning.
The people who understood the
stories learned more about God.
Do you like to read stories?
The stories Jesus told are in
the Bible.
You can read them.
They are good stories!

TODAY'S WORD

stories

PRAYER

Dear Jesus,
thank You for
Your stories in
the Bible. They will
help me to learn
more about You.
In Jesus' name,
amen.

"I, your Lord and Teacher, have washed your feet. So you also should wash each other's feet." —John 13:14

Wash Your Feet

TODAY'S WORD

feet

Do you wash your hands before you eat?
Do you wash your feet?
In Bible times, people walked on dusty roads.
Their feet got dirty.
When they went to someone's home, a servant would wash their feet.
One night Jesus and His followers were having a special meal.
Jesus washed everyone's feet.
He did this to show His followers that we need to serve others.

PRAYER

Thank You, Jesus, for being a good example. Help me to serve others too. In Jesus' name, amen.

He made the storm as quiet as a whisper. The waves of the ocean calmed down. —Psalm 107:29 NIrV

Quiet as a Whisper

God is great and powerful.

He can make it thunder.

He can make the wind blow hard.

And He can stop a storm.

The Bible says that God can make

the waves as quiet as a whisper.

The wind and waves obey God's voice.

Sometimes His voice is loud

like thunder.

Sometimes it is quiet like

a whisper.

If the wind and waves obey God,

we should obey Him too.

PRAYER

Dear God. You are so powerful. You can do anything. Help me to obey You like the wind and waves. In Jesus' name, amen.

175

BIBLE VERSE

Share with God's people who are in need. Welcome others into your homes.
—Romans 12:13 NIrV

Welcome Others

TODAY'S WORD

welcome

Do you like having friends
over to play?
Your home is a special place for
your family.
It is also a special place for
your friends.
Jesus wants us to welcome others
into our homes and share with them.
You can share your toys or a snack.
You can read books together
or listen to music.
When you welcome others into your
home, they will want to come back.

PRAYER

Dear Jesus, thank
You for my home and
family. Help me to
share my home with
others. In Jesus'
name, amen.

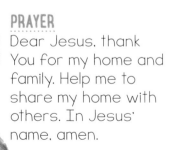

You will understand what is honest and fair and right. You will understand what is good to do. —Proverbs 2:9

Understand It

Your teachers want you to understand what they teach you in school.
Your parents want you to understand what they teach you at home.
God wants you to understand His words in the Bible.
He wants you to understand that He loves you.
He wants you to understand how to treat others.
Ask God to help you understand His words in the Bible.
And He will.

TODAY'S WORD

understand

PRAYER

Dear God, thank You for the Bible. Help me to understand Your words. In Jesus' name, amen.

177

Serve the Lord with joy. —Psalm 100:2

Serve with Joy

TODAY'S WORD
serve

Serving others means to help them. When you serve others, it shows that you love them.

You can serve your mom by making your bed.

You can serve your dad by helping him clean up the yard.

You can serve others by being kind.

When you serve others, you are also serving God.

There are many ways to serve.

God wants you to serve with joy.

PRAYER

Dear God, please help me to serve others with joy. In Jesus' name, amen.

Let the hearts of those who seek the LORD rejoice. —Psalm 105:3 NIV

Seek God

Some people seek money.
They want to be rich.
Some people seek fame.
They want to be famous.
Some people seek to be popular.
They want everyone to like them.
People think that being rich or
famous or popular will make
them happy.
But seeking God is the most
important thing to do.
When you seek God, you will
be happy.

TODAY'S WORD

seek

PRAYER
Dear God, help me to seek You more than
anything else. I know that will make me happy. In
Jesus' name, amen.

The Lord Keeps You

TODAY'S WORD

keep

Do you have something special
that you keep in a safe place?
Maybe someone gave you a special
gift that is important to you.
People keep important and special
things in a safe place.
Did you know that you are important
and special to God?
He loves you and wants to keep
you safe.
He will keep you forever!

PRAYER

Dear God, thank You that You love me
and keep me safe. Thank You that
I am important to You. In Jesus'
name, amen.

When I called out to you, you answered me. You made me strong and brave.
—Psalm 138:3 NIrV

God Will Answer

David was a shepherd boy.
He loved God very much.
Sometimes a big animal would
come after his sheep.
David would pray to God right away.
God would always answer him.
God would help David to be
strong and brave.
You can pray to God just like
David did.
God will always answer you.
He will help you to be strong
and brave.

TODAY'S WORD

answer

PRAYER

Dear God, thank You that You
answer me when I pray to You.
Help me to be strong and brave. In
Jesus' name, amen.

God's Riches

TODAY'S WORD

riches

Some people have big homes.

Some people have fancy cars.

Some people have many clothes.

Those things are nice for a while.

But they don't last.

God has riches that will

last forever.

He will give you all that you need.

God's riches make us happy.

God's riches give us peace.

God's riches come to us

through Jesus.

When you believe in Jesus,

God shares all His riches with you.

PRAYER

Dear God, thank You for sharing Your riches with me. In Jesus' name, amen.

The Best Choice

Joshua was one of the leaders of God's people.

He wanted the people to serve God.

Some of the people served false gods.

Joshua told the people to choose whom they would serve.

Joshua chose to serve God.

Many of the people said they would choose to serve God too.

Today we still get to choose whom we will serve.

Choose to serve God.

It's the best choice.

TODAY'S WORD

choose

PRAYER
Dear God. I will choose to serve You. I know that is the best choice. In Jesus' name, amen.

You Belong

Have you ever put your name on something important that belongs to you?

Maybe you put your name on your books or your baseball cap.

Did you know you are important?

You belong to your family.

You have your family's name.

You also belong to God.

When you believe in Jesus,

He puts His name on you.

You are important to Him.

PRAYER

Dear Jesus, thank You that I can belong to You. I am happy that I am important to You. Amen.

Now there is a crown waiting for me. It is given to those who are right with God. —2 Timothy 4:8 NIrV

A Crown for You

TODAY'S WORD

crown

A king wears a crown to show
that he is a king.
It is called a royal crown.
Someday you will get a crown too.
Everyone who loves God and believes
in Jesus will get a crown.
Someday Jesus will come back.
He will have a crown for His people.
It will be better than a
royal crown.
It will be a crown that
lasts forever.

PRAYER

Dear God, thank You that You will give
me a crown someday. I want to be in
Your kingdom. In Jesus' name, amen.

All the Same

TODAY'S WORD

same

Boys are different from girls.

Men are different from women.

Kids are different from grown-ups.

No one is exactly the same.

Even though we are all different,

there is something that is the same.

Do you know what that is?

Jesus sees us all the same.

He cares for us all the same.

He loves us all the same.

And Jesus has enough love

for everyone.

PRAYER

Dear Jesus, thank You that You love us all the same and that You have enough love for us all. In Jesus' name, amen.

A friend loves you all the time. A brother is always there to help you.
—Proverbs 17:17

All the Time

Jesus loves us all the time.
Whether we are happy or sad,
His love for us never changes.
He always loves us no matter what.
Jesus wants us to love others that
way too.
If your friend is having a bad day,
love him anyway.
If your brother or sister is sad,
love them anyway.
Always love others.
That's what Jesus does.

TODAY'S WORD

always

PRAYER

Dear Jesus, thank You that You always love me.
Help me to always love others too. In Jesus'
name, amen.

God's Idea

God had an idea to make the world.

So He did.

The sun, moon, and stars
were God's idea.

The land and sea were God's idea.

The animals were God's idea.

And while God was making His world,

He thought about making you.

He planned when you would be born.

He wanted you to be a part of
His big, beautiful world.

You were God's idea too!

PRAYER

Dear God, thank You for creating Your wonderful world. Thank You for wanting me to be a part of it. In Jesus' name, amen.

"When the rainbow appears in the clouds, I will see it. Then I will remember the agreement that continues forever." —Genesis 9:16

Rainbows and Promises

Do you know the colors of
the rainbow?
Red is the first color at the top.
Then comes orange, yellow, green,
blue, indigo, and violet.
The first rainbow appeared after
the Flood.
It was a sign from God.
He promised to never flood the
earth again.
When we see a rainbow, it reminds
us of God's promise.
The rainbow is beautiful.
So is God's promise!

PRAYER

Dear God, thank You for making rainbows and promises. In Jesus' name, amen.

"Look at the flowers of the field. See how they grow." —Matthew 6:28

Thousands of Flowers

TODAY'S WORD

flowers

What is your favorite flower?
Is it a rose or a tulip?
Is it a daisy or a buttercup?
Can you guess how many different
kinds of flowers there are?
There are more than one hundred.
There are more than one thousand.
There are more than ten thousand
different kinds of flowers!
Flowers are pretty.
They smell nice too!
God made thousands of flowers
for us to enjoy.

PRAYER

Dear God, thank You for making all the flowers that make our world so beautiful. In Jesus' name, amen.

That prize is mine because God called me through Christ to the life above.
—Philippians 3:14

The Best Prize

Have you ever won a prize?
Some people win prizes for
running a race.
Some people win prizes for
painting a picture.
Kids can get a prize for
winning a spelling bee.
There are many ways to win prizes.
Paul was a follower of Jesus.
He worked hard telling others
about Jesus.
He knew that someday he would be
with Jesus in heaven.
That's the best prize of all!

TODAY'S WORD

prize

PRAYER

Dear Jesus, thank You that I can have the prize of
being with You in heaven. In Jesus' name, amen.

191

We are like clay, and you are the potter. Your hands made us all.
—Isaiah 64:8

In the Potter's Hands

potter

Have you ever made anything out of clay?

It is fun to shape and mold something using clay.

A person who makes things out of clay is called a potter.

The Bible says that God is our Potter.

He shapes us and molds us into the people He wants us to be.

God's hands are gentle and loving.

It's good to be in the Potter's hands.

PRAYER

Dear God, thank You that You are my Potter. Make me to be the person You want me to be. In Jesus' name, amen.

As for God, his way is perfect: The LORD's word is flawless.
—Psalm 18:30 NIV

Our Perfect God

Have you ever heard the saying
"nobody's perfect"?
It's true that no person is perfect.
But God is perfect.
Everything about God is perfect.
His love is perfect.
His ways are perfect.
His words in the Bible are perfect.
That is why we can believe what
we read in the Bible.
That is why we can trust God.
Nobody's perfect.
But God is.

TODAY'S WORD

perfect

PRAYER

Dear God, I am thankful that You are a perfect God. I know I can believe in You and Your Word. In Jesus' name, amen.

Do everything for the glory of God. —1 Corinthians 10:31

Give Glory to God

The Bible tells us to give
glory to God.
It means to honor Him.
It means to show God that we love
Him by the things we do.
We can give glory to God when
we sing songs to Him.
We can give glory to God when
we pray.
We can give glory to God by
being kind.
When we do our best for God,
it gives Him glory.

PRAYER

Dear God, help me to do everything for Your
glory. In Jesus' name, amen.

Praise him with stringed instruments and flutes. —Psalm 150:4

Instruments of Praise

People use instruments to
make music.
Some people play songs on the
piano or guitar.
Did you know that
people in Bible times had
instruments too?
They had instruments made
with strings.
They had horns they could blow.
They used their instruments to
praise God just like we do today.
If you learn to play an instrument,
you can use it to praise God.

PRAYER

Dear God, thank You for
instruments and music and
songs. I like to praise You.
In Jesus' name, amen.

195

Mightier than the thunder of the great waters, mightier than the breakers of the sea—the LORD on high is mighty. —Psalm 93:4 NIV

Our Mighty God

TODAY'S WORD

mighty

The waves of an ocean are powerful
and mighty.
They can crash against the rocks.
They can splash on the shore.
They can toss and turn with
the wind.
Sometimes they sound like a roar.
Sometimes they sound like thunder.
They are mighty to look at.
They are mighty to hear.
God created the ocean with its
mighty waves and mighty roar.
He is a mighty God.

PRAYER

Dear God, You are a mighty God. Thank You for being my God. In Jesus' name, amen.

The LORD directs the steps of the godly. He delights in every detail of their lives. —Psalm 37:23 NLT

The Right Direction

When someone takes a step in the right direction, it means they made a good decision.

The Bible tells us that God directs the steps of His children.

That means He will guide you and help you know what to do.

God cares about you and all the decisions you have to make.

Ask God to direct your steps. He will help you to take steps in the right direction.

PRAYER

Dear God, please direct my steps so I can do what You want me to do. In Jesus' name, amen.

BIBLE VERSE

You also became believers in Christ. That happened when you heard the message of truth. It was the good news about how you could be saved. —Ephesians 1:13 NIrV

A True Message

People get lots of messages.
You can get them on a phone.
You can hear them on TV.
A friend can give you a message too.
Some messages are true, but some
might not be true.
The most important message
is about Jesus.
The Bible says that believing in
Jesus is the way we can be saved.
You can believe that message!
The Bible's messages are true!

PRAYER

Dear God, thank You for the messages in the Bible. I know they are true. In Jesus' name, amen.

"If a person remains in me and I in him, then he produces much fruit."
—John 15:5

Good Fruit

Have you ever picked fruit
from a tree?
Fruit hangs from the branches,
which are connected to the trunk.
If a branch is separated from the
trunk, it cannot grow fruit.
Jesus says we are like branches.
If we stay connected to Him,
we can grow fruit.
Jesus is talking about the good
things we do like being kind
and helping others.
That kind of fruit always
tastes good!

TODAY'S WORD
fruit

PRAYER

Dear Jesus, please help me to grow good fruit by
being kind and helpful. In Jesus' name, amen.

I pray that the God who gives hope will fill you with much joy and peace while you trust in him. —Romans 15:13

Hope for Good Things

hope

People hope for good things.

They hope for a good job.

They hope for a good family.

They hope for joy and happiness.

Did you ever hope for something?

God wants us to talk to Him about the things we hope for.

When we believe in God, we can have lots of hope.

God gives us hope and joy and peace all at the same time!

PRAYER

Dear God, thank You that I can hope for good things because You love me. In Jesus' name, amen.

BIBLE VERSE

Now Jesus is Prince and Savior. God has proved this by giving him a place of honor at his own right hand. —Acts 5:31 NIrV

The Greatest Prince

The son of a king is called
a prince.
A prince lives in the king's palace.
Did you know that Jesus is called
a prince?
That's because He is the Son of God.
God is our King.
He rules over the whole world.
Jesus rules with Him in heaven.
Jesus saves people who believe
in Him.
No other prince can do that.
Jesus is the greatest Prince of all.

PRAYER

Dear Jesus, You are the Son of God. You are the Prince who saves people from sin. In Jesus' name, amen.

BIBLE VERSE

He gathers the people like lambs in his arms. He carries them close to him.
—Isaiah 40:11

In His Arms

TODAY'S WORD

gather

A shepherd takes good care of his sheep.
He gathers them together so he can watch over them.
Sometimes he has to carry a lamb that is hurt or lost.
The shepherd holds the lamb in his arms and carries it close to him.
The Bible says that God loves us the same way.
He gathers His people together.
He holds us in His arms and keeps us close.

PRAYER

Dear God, thank You that You love us and keep us close to You. In Jesus' name, amen.

Ask God Anything

Did you know you can ask
God anything?
You can ask God to help you
at school.
You can ask God to help your
mom or dad at work.
You can ask God to help you
to be healthy and strong.
You can ask God to give
you wisdom.
You can ask God to keep you safe.
So go ahead and ask Him anything.
He already knows what you need!

TODAY'S WORD

ask

PRAYER

Dear God, I am glad that You
know what I need. Thank
You that I can ask You
for anything. In Jesus'
name, amen.

203

BIBLE VERSE

I wait for the Lord to help me. I trust his word. —Psalm 130:5

Time to Wait

TODAY'S WORD

wait

It's hard to wait for your birthday.
It's hard to wait for Christmas.
When we look forward to something,
it can be hard to wait.
Have you ever asked God for
something and then you had to
wait for His answer?
God always hears your prayers.
But sometimes we need to wait for
His answer.
God knows what is best.
He will answer your
prayer when
the time is right.

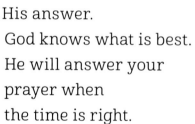

PRAYER

Dear God, You know what
is best. Help me to wait for
You and trust You. In Jesus'
name, amen.

Use Your Voice

Did you know you can honor God
with your voice?
You can use your voice to say kind
words to others.
You can use your voice to pray.
You can use your voice to
sing praises.
You can use your voice to say
a Bible verse.
There are many ways you can use
your voice to honor God.
And God hears every word you say!

TODAY'S WORD

voice

PRAYER

Dear God, thank You that You hear my voice. Help me
to use my voice to honor You. In Jesus' name, amen.

Filled with Wonder

TODAY'S WORD

wonder

One day Jesus was in a house filled with people.

Some men cut a hole in the roof.

They lowered a man down in front of Jesus.

The man could not walk.

Jesus told him to get up and walk.

And just like that, the man stood up and walked!

He praised God all the way home.

The people were filled with wonder.

Everyone gave praise to God.

PRAYER

Dear Jesus, You are so great. You can heal sick people. You can do many great things! In Jesus' name, amen.

206

The LORD takes delight in his people. —Psalm 149:4 NIrV

The Lord's Delight

Do you enjoy a glass of lemonade
on a hot day?
Do you enjoy a cozy bed when
you are sleepy?
Do you like holding a little kitten?
Things that we enjoy give
us delight.
They make us happy inside.
Do you know what gives God delight?
You do!
God delights in people who love Him.
Tell God that you love Him today.
He will delight in you!

PRAYER

Dear God, I am glad that You
delight in people who love You. You
are a great God! I love You because
You love me! In Jesus' name, amen.

To know [Jesus] is the best thing of all. –Philippians 3:8 NIrV

The Best Thing

It's good to have a good family.

It's good to have good friends.

It's good to be strong.

It's good to be happy.

It's good to be wise.

But the best thing in the whole
world is to know Jesus.

Jesus gives us everything we need.

He is our friend.

He loves us.

He saves us.

He gives us joy.

He is the best!

PRAYER

Dear Jesus, I want to know You more and more.
Knowing You is better than anything. In Jesus'
name, amen.

Running Over

Did you ever pour too much
milk into a cup?
If you pour too much milk,
it will run down the sides.
You will have more milk than you need.
The Bible says that God gives us
more blessings than we need.
He loves us so much that He pours
His blessings on us.
It's like having a cup that
keeps running over.

TODAY'S WORD

cup

PRAYER

Dear God, thank
You for all the many
blessings You give
to me. You keep
giving me more
and more every
day. In Jesus'
name, amen.

Stir It Up

TODAY'S WORD

stir

People at a football game stir
each other up.
When one person starts to cheer,
it makes other people cheer.
Soon the whole crowd is cheering!
That is what Christians can do when
they show love to others.
They can stir others up to love each
other and help each other.
All it takes is one person to
get started.
Pretty soon, others will join in.

PRAYER

Dear God, help me to show love to others so
others will show love too. In Jesus' name, amen.

Let the heavens be full of joy. Let the earth be glad. Let the ocean and everything in it roar. —Psalm 96:11 NIrV

Sounds of Creation

God created a beautiful world.

He created people to enjoy His world.

Everything God created praises Him.

The birds sing His praises.

The tree toads hum His praises.

The sun brings joy as it shines
on the earth.

The wind blows gentle praises
through the trees.

The ocean waves roar with praise to God.

Everything gives praise to God.

You can praise God too!

PRAYER

Dear God, everything
You made gives praise to
You. I will praise You too.
In Jesus' name, amen.

My teaching will drop like rain. My words will fall like dew. They will be like showers on the grass. —Deuteronomy 32:2

Words Like Rain

TODAY'S WORD

grass

Have you ever looked at the grass after it rains?
Grass is greener after it rains.
Grass grows better after it rains.
Without rain, grass would dry up.
God's words in the Bible are like raindrops for His people.
God's words help us to grow closer to Him.
His teachings make us brighter.
Just like the grass needs rain, we need to read God's words.

PRAYER
Dear God, thank You for Your words in the Bible. I know they will help me to grow closer to You. In Jesus' name, amen.

Jesus led his disciples out to the area near Bethany. Then he lifted up his hands and blessed them. —Luke 24:50 NIrV

Lift Up Your Hands

TODAY'S WORD
hands

Jesus said good-bye to His followers
before He went back to heaven.
He lifted up His hands and
blessed them.
Then He went into the clouds.
We can lift up our hands just like
Jesus did.
We can lift our hands when we pray.
We can lift our hands when we sing.
We can lift up our hands and point
to Jesus in heaven.

PRAYER

Dear Jesus, thank You that I can lift my hands
toward heaven to sing and pray to You. In Jesus'
name, amen.

Give me understanding so I can learn your commands. —Psalm 119:73

Keep Learning

You can learn many things.

You can learn to read and write.

You can learn to spell.

You can learn to do math problems.

The more you learn, the more
you will know.

You can also learn many things
about God.

The Bible helps us to learn
how He wants us to live.

There is no end to what you
can learn about God.

So keep learning!

PRAYER

Dear God, please help me to learn more and
more about You. In Jesus' name, amen.

Look to the LORD and to his strength. Always look to him.
—Psalm 105:4 NIrV

Look the Right Way

When you cross a street, you have
to look both ways.
When you go down the stairs, you
need to look at the stairs.
Looking the right way keeps
you safe.
Looking to God keeps you safe too.
You can look to Him when you pray.
You can look to Him when you read
the Bible.
Looking to God is always the right
way to look!

PRAYER

Dear God, help
me to always
look to You. I
know You will
help me with
whatever I
need. In Jesus'
name, amen.

We are full of joy because we expect to share in God's glory.
—Romans 5:2 NIrV

Expect Good Things

You expect to see animals when you go to the zoo.

You expect to see other kids when you go to school.

You expect to see food when you go to the grocery store.

Did you know you can expect things from God? If you love God, you can expect Him to share His blessings with you. And you can expect Him to love you forever!

PRAYER

Dear God, thank You for all the blessings I have because of Your love for me. In Jesus' name, amen.

He is a faithful God who does no wrong. He is right and fair.
—Deuteronomy 32:4

God Is Always Fair

Did you ever hear someone say,
"That's not fair!"?
We like it when things are fair.
We want our teachers to be fair.
We want our parents to be fair.
We want our friends to be fair.
Did you know that God is fair?
God is perfect.
He is always right.
And God is always fair.
You can trust that God will
be fair every day!

TODAY'S WORD
fair

PRAYER
Dear God, thank
You that You
are always
right and
always fair.
In Jesus'
name, amen.

Jesus said . . . , "Don't be afraid; from now on you will fish for people."
—Luke 5:10 NIV

Jesus and the Fishermen

Jesus was talking to some fishermen.
They had not caught any fish.
Jesus told them to try again.
This time they caught more than
their nets could hold!
The fishermen were surprised!
Jesus told the fishermen to
follow Him.
He said they would fish for people.
Jesus meant they would find
more people to be His followers.
So they followed Jesus and
began to fish for people.

PRAYER
Dear Jesus, I can fish for people
too. Help me to tell my friends
about You. In Jesus' name, amen.

So they hurried off and found Mary and Joseph and the baby.
—Luke 2:16 NIrV

Hurry to Jesus

On the night that Jesus was born,
an angel told the shepherds where
they could find Jesus.
The shepherds didn't waste any time.
They hurried as fast as they could!
They ran all the way until they
found Jesus.
You can hurry to Jesus too.
When you want to talk to Him,
you can go to Him right away.
Don't waste any time.
Hurry to Him today!

TODAY'S WORD
hurry

PRAYER
Dear Jesus, thank You that I can hurry to You
and You will always be there to talk to. In Jesus'
name, amen.

Let your ears listen to wisdom. Apply your heart to understanding.
—Proverbs 2:2 NIrV

Use Your Ears

You can use your ears to listen
to a train.
You can use your ears to listen
to a story or a song.
The Bible tells us to use our ears
to listen to wisdom.
That means to listen to people who
tell you wise things.
When grown-ups teach you lessons
from the Bible, it's good to listen!

PRAYER

Dear God, please help me to listen to wise words
from the Bible. In Jesus' name, amen.

Who has measured the oceans in the palm of his hand? Who has used his hand to measure the sky. —Isaiah 40:12

Measure the Sky

Do you ever measure how tall you are?

Do you use a tape measure

or a yardstick?

People measure many things.

But they could never measure the ocean.

They could never measure the sky.

Only God can do that.

God doesn't need a yardstick.

He doesn't need a tape measure.

God uses His hand to measure

the ocean and the sky.

TODAY'S WORD

measure

PRAYER

Dear God, You are great! Only You can measure the ocean and the sky with Your hand. In Jesus' name, amen.

221

A Happy Mouth

TODAY'S WORD

mouth

Do you know how you can have a happy mouth?

You can smile a big smile.

You can blow a bubble.

You can whisper something sweet.

You can laugh.

You can give your mom a kiss on the cheek.

You can use your mouth to say words that please God. Think about things that please God.

Then your words will please Him too.

Have a happy mouth!

PRAYER

Dear God, please help my thoughts and words be pleasing to You. In Jesus' name, amen.

"Where two or three people meet together in my name, I am there with them." —Matthew 18:20 NIrV

Meet with Jesus

Do you meet with other boys and
girls at church or Sunday school?
Do you read the Bible with your
family around the table?
When you meet with others to talk
about Jesus, He is right there.
Jesus wants to be a part of your meeting.
He listens to your words.
He helps you to understand more
about Him.
When you meet with others, meet
with Jesus too.

TODAY'S WORD

meet

PRAYER

Dear Jesus, thank You that You are with me when
I meet with others to talk about You. In Jesus'
name, amen.

God's Goodness

God's goodness is great.

He gives good things to His people.

Because of His goodness,

He keeps us safe.

He gives us more than we need.

He is with us every day and night.

He loves us.

He gives us our family and friends.

He blesses us every day with

good things.

God's goodness lasts forever.

PRAYER

Dear God, You do so many good things for me. Thank You for Your goodness. In Jesus' name, amen.

Everyone Who Believes

TODAY'S WORD

everyone

Who are the people in your family?
Your parents are in your family.
Your grandparents are in
your family.
If you have brothers or sisters,
they are in your family too.
You might have some good friends,
but they are in another family.
In God's family, it is different.
Everyone who believes in Jesus
is in God's family.
They are all God's children.
Everyone!

PRAYER

Dear God, I am happy that everyone who believes
in Jesus is in Your family. In Jesus' name, amen.

Let us keep looking to Jesus. —Hebrews 12:2 NIrV

Looking to Jesus

You have many things to look at.
You can look at books.
You can look at a computer.
You can look at magazines.
You can look at the clouds.
But the best thing to look
at is Jesus.
You can learn from Him.
He teaches us how to live.
He teaches us how to love.
He lived a perfect life.
So keep looking to Jesus.

PRAYER

Dear Jesus, please help me to keep looking to You so I can learn from You. In Jesus' name, amen.

[God] wanted us to be the most important of all the things he made.
—James 1:18

The Most Important

God used words to create the world.

He said, "Let there be light."

And there was light.

He used words to create the sun,

moon, and stars.

He used words to create trees

and animals.

But when God created man,

He used His hands.

He formed man from the ground.

God breathed life into him.

God saw that all He had made was good.

But people were the most important.

PRAYER

Dear God, thank You that I am so important to You.
Thank You for creating me. In Jesus' name, amen.

Taste and See

TODAY'S WORD

taste

Apples taste good.
But you have to eat them in order
to know how they taste.
Honey is sweet.
But you have to taste it in order
to know how sweet it is.
God is good.
How can you know?
You can pray to God.
You can read His words in the Bible.
Spend time with God.
Then you will know how good He is.

PRAYER

Dear God, I know that You are good. Help me to know You more by spending time with You. In Jesus' name, amen.

Jesus has the power of God. His power has given us everything we need to live and to serve God. —2 Peter 1:3

Jesus' Power

When Jesus lived on the earth,
He healed people with His power.
Jesus has power because He is God.
Jesus' power is for us too.
His power will help us to love others.
His power will help us to live the
way God wants us to.
His power will help us to do
our best.
His power is the greatest power
there is.

PRAYER
Dear Jesus, thank You that Your power helps me to do my best for You. In Jesus' name, amen.

When the name of Jesus is spoken, everyone's knee will bow to worship him. —Philippians 2:10 NIrV

Everyone's Knee Will Bow

TODAY'S WORD

bow

Jesus is living in heaven.
But we can talk to Him in prayer.
Even though we can't see Him,
He is with us every day.
He helps us with our problems.
He helps us to be strong.
Someday, Jesus is coming back.
Everyone will see Him.
At the sound of His name,
everyone will bow down.
Everyone will worship Him.
It is going to be a
wonderful day!

PRAYER

Dear Jesus, someday everyone will bow down and worship You. Thank You that I can worship You every day. In Jesus' name, amen.

Blessed is the nation whose God is the LORD. —Psalm 33:12 NIrV

Bless the Nations

Nation is another word for *country*.
In the Bible, God says that He will
bless the nations that obey Him.
He will bless the nations that love
Him and serve Him.
God keeps His promises.
When nations love and serve God,
He blesses them.
God will bless our nation too
if we love and serve God.
Pray for God to bless our nation.

PRAYER
Dear God, please bless our nation. I pray that
our people would love and serve You. In Jesus'
name, amen.

The one who plants a lot will gather a lot. —2 Corinthians 9:6 NIrV

Planting Seeds

A farmer plants wheat seeds to grow wheat.
The more seeds he plants, the more wheat he will grow.
The same thing is true in our lives.
We can plant seeds of love and kindness.
We can plant seeds of helping and giving.
Those kind of seeds always grow into good things.
The more seeds we plant, the more good things will grow.

PRAYER

Dear God, please help me to plant seeds of love and kindness. In Jesus' name, amen.

232

The Lord will guard you as you come and go, both now and forever.
—Psalm 121:8

God Is Our Guard

The president has someone who stays
by his side to keep him safe.
That person is called a bodyguard.
The bodyguard goes with him
everywhere he goes.
God is like a bodyguard.
He stays by your side.
He keeps you safe.
He will guard you wherever you go.
He is stronger than any person.
He is stronger than any guard.
He will be your guard forever.

TODAY'S WORD

guard

PRAYER

Dear God, thank You for being my guard and keeping me safe. I am glad You are always with me. In Jesus' name, amen.

BIBLE VERSE

Know and believe today that the Lord is God. He is God in heaven above and on the earth below. There is no other god! —Deuteronomy 4:39

Know and Believe

When you believe something,
that means you know it is true.
You can believe that birds fly
because you know it is true.
You can believe that fish swim
because you know it is true.
Do you know what else you
can believe?
You can believe that God is the only
God in heaven and earth.
The Bible tells us it's true.
You can know it and believe it!

PRAYER
Dear God, I know and believe that You are the only God. In Jesus' name, amen.

Every good and perfect gift is from God. It comes down from the Father. —James 1:17 NIrV

Gifts from Above

Gifts that come from a store
are not always perfect.
A shirt can be too big.
Shoes can be too small.
Sometimes that happens when
people give gifts.
God's gifts come from heaven.
He gives us food and sunshine.
He gives us pretty flowers.
He gives us Jesus.
He gives us His love.
Every gift from God is good.
Every gift from God is perfect.

TODAY'S WORD

every

PRAYER

Dear God, thank You for Your good and perfect gifts. In Jesus' name, amen.

They will not need the light of a lamp or the light of the sun. The Lord God will give them light. —Revelation 22:5

Always Bright

TODAY'S WORD

bright

Can you imagine what it would be
like if it never got dark?
That is what heaven is like.
It is always bright in heaven
because God is there.

Heaven doesn't need the sun.
Heaven doesn't need lights.
God is light.
He is brighter than the sun.
He is brighter than the
brightest lights.
God makes every-
thing bright.

PRAYER

Dear God, thank You
that You make everything
bright. You are the light of the
world. In Jesus' name, amen.

"In that day you will ask the Father for things in my name."
—John 16:26

In Jesus' Name

Jesus told His followers that
one day soon they would pray
to God in Jesus' name.
That day came when Jesus
died on the cross for our sins.
When we believe in Jesus,
our sins are forgiven.
Jesus is the way to God.
So when we pray to God,
we pray in Jesus' name.
You can pray in Jesus' name
every day.

TODAY'S WORD

day

PRAYER

Dear God, thank You for sending Jesus to forgive
my sins. I know I can pray to You because of
Jesus. In Jesus' name, amen.

"The greatest love a person can show is to die for his friends."
—John 15:13

The Greatest Love

God created us because He loves us.

God watches over us because He loves us.

God gives us blessings because He loves us.

God sent Jesus to die for our sins
because He loves us.

Jesus died so we can go to heaven.

That is the greatest love there is.

You can tell others about God's love.

You can thank God for His love.

God's love is the greatest.

PRAYER

Dear God. Your love for me is so great. Thank You for Jesus, the greatest love of all. In Jesus' name, amen.

239

Crystal Bowman is an award-winning author of over 75 books for children, including *The One Year Book of Devotions for Preschoolers*, *My Grandma and Me*, and *J is for Jesus*. She is a speaker for MOPS (Mothers of Preschoolers) and teaches at writers conferences. Whether her stories are written in playful rhyme or short sentences, Crystal hopes kids will want to read them again and again. A mother and grandmother, Crystal lives in Florida with her husband.

Christy Lee Taylor has long been involved in the arts. With a background in acting and modeling, she founded Abba Productions, Inc. Her first film as a producer was the family film *Turkles*, which won multiple awards. She speaks at many events and works with children in teaching and coaching roles. Christy won an award for a picture book series at the Florida Christian Writers Conference in 2011. She and her husband live in Florida with their son and twin daughters.